Baby Tips®

Baby's First Year

Baby Tips®

Baby's First Year

by Jeanne Murphy

FISHER
BOOKS™
FOR HEALTHY LIVING™

Publishers: Helen V. Fisher, Howard W. Fisher

Managing Editor: Sarah Trotta

Editor: Melanie Mallon

Illustrations: Cathie Lowmiller

Book design
& Production: Randy Schultz

Cover design: Lynn Bishop

Published by Fisher Books, LLC
5225 W. Massingale Road
Tucson, Arizona 85743-8416
(520) 744-6110
www.fisherbooks.com

**Library of Congress
Cataloging-in-Publication Data**
Murphy, Jeanne, 1964-
   Baby's first year / Jeanne Murphy.
      p. cm.
   Includes index.
   ISBN 1-55561-240-7
   1. Infants—Care.
   2. Infants—Health and hygiene.
   3. Parenting. 4. Child rearing.
   I. Title.

RJ131 .M87 2000
649'.122—dc21   00-023763

Printed and bound in Canada
10 9 8 7 6 5 4 3 2 1

Note: The information in this book is true and complete to the best of
our knowledge. It is offered with no guarantees on the part of the author
or Fisher Books. The author and publisher disclaim all liability in
connection with the use of this book.

The suggestions in this book are opinions and are not meant to
supersede a doctor's recommendation in any way. Always consult
your doctor before beginning any new program.

Dedication

This book is dedicated to my husband, Jan, who's given me two perfect children, and to my parents, Bel-Mehr and Beaupa. Their real names are Judy and Mike, but they changed them to entertain the grandchildren. That's just one of the many things I love about them!

Table of Contents

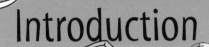

Introduction

This is a true story. One day I went to the doctor's office because my baby required his immunization shots. While I sat in the examination room, the doctor came in and said, "Jeanne, I really enjoyed reading your books and I recommend them to new parents." And then he said, "I don't really know you that well, but are you a doctor?"

"No."

"Oh, then are you a nurse?"

"No."

"Did you always want to write a book?"

"No."

And then he asked, "Well, where did you get all your information?"

"I am a mother."

About This Book
Note from the publisher

No doubt, throughout your pregnancy, you've received advice from all sides: friends, relatives, doctors, nurses, childbirth-education and parenting classes, and scores of books on every subject imaginable related to becoming and being a good parent. This book is not meant to replace that advice. Nor is it meant to be a comprehensive encyclopedia of everything you will ever encounter during your baby's first year—after all, what busy new parent has time to wade through that much information?

Instead, this book is intended as a quick reference, full of tips, checklists, forms and anecdotes, to supplement the advice you've already received. Looking for help with feeding your new little one? Thumb through the Feeding and Changing chapter for quick bites of tried-and-true techniques. Or perhaps you've got that down and really need advice on how to care for your child's health—skip to the Health chapter for wisdom and reassurance.

And what new parent couldn't use tips for saving time and money? Look for the clock and dollar sign icons throughout the book, pointing you to invaluable advice for making the most of those valuable resources. Also keep an eye out for the fairy icon, which indicates tips for keeping yourself sane, and the red cross icon, which indicates tips for avoiding hazards and keeping baby safe.

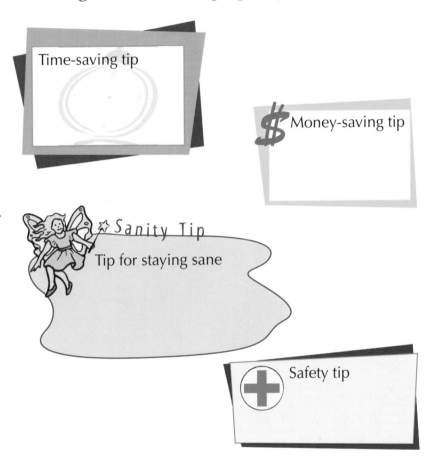

Time-saving tip

Money-saving tip

Sanity Tip
Tip for staying sane

Safety tip

Keep a copy of this book in the nursery or in your diaper bag and you'll always have somewhere to turn when you need a little help—and you need it now—or simply when you need a little reassurance or humor to keep you going while doing the world's toughest—and most rewarding—job: being a parent!

Equipment and Safety Checklists

Nothing can make the job of a new parent easier than being prepared. Following are two checklists to get you started before you even bring home your new bundle of joy. Even if you've already brought baby home, it doesn't hurt to double-check that you have all the equipment and supplies you'll need and that you've done everything possible to make your home safe for the new addition.

Baby Equipment

Essential:

❏ Baby monitor
❏ Crib
❏ Stroller
❏ Car seat/carrier seat
❏ Highchair
❏ Portable fan
❏ Activity center
❏ Portable playpen—"playyard"
❏ Thermometer (rectal)
❏ Baby nail clippers
❏ Diapers (cloth or disposable)
❏ Diaper pins and plastic pants (for cloth)
❏ Changing table or mat

- Cotton balls
- Diaper wipes
- Diaper cream
- Crib sheets
- Cotton swabs
- Bibs
- Hat
- Socks
- First-aid kit (These are sold as complete kits, but ask your doctor what should be included so that you buy the best kit.)
- Baby tub
- Baby washcloths
- Vaporizer

Strongly recommended:

- Second monitor
- Bouncing seat
- Swing
- Jumping device (the kind that hangs from your doorframe)
- Device that will allow your baby to play sitting in an upright position, such as the new walkers with safety wheels to prevent tipping or falling down stairs.
- Thermometer (ear)
- Diaper pail (for disposable)

continued . . .

- ❑ Receiving blanket
- ❑ Undershirts (one-piece shirts that snap between legs are best)
- ❑ Stretchy jumpsuits with feet (slightly big for baby)
- ❑ Baby slings (depends completely on the type of parent you are)
- ❑ Rattles
- ❑ Dresser

Not essential, but handy:

- ❑ Waterproof pads (for crib)
- ❑ Wipe-warmers (or just warm them up in your hand)
- ❑ Bottle-warmers (Hot water in a cup works just as well. The milk doesn't last more than two hours if you use a bottle warmer, so then you're kept awake at night worrying if the milk or formula is good.)
- ❑ Massage oil
- ❑ Hooded towels

Baby-Proof Your Home

❑ Remove or fix any pavement or floorboard that isn't level—these are trip hazards for everyone.

❑ Check baseboards for wooden splinters.

❑ Put loose change in a designated, *out-of-reach* place. (Remember: When baby starts pulling herself up, she'll be able to reach above her head.)

❑ Secure all doors and drawers (closet, cabinet, screen and so on).

❑ Cover all outlets not in use with child-proof covers and don't leave any plugs or cords lying around.

❑ Install baby-proof latches on cabinets and drawers.

❑ Install safety door-knob covers.

❑ Tablecloths—simply remove these for a while.

❑ Do not put pillows, stuffed animals or thick bedding in the crib or your baby is at greater risk for SIDS and suffocation.

❑ Lay rugs or thick carpeting under crib and changing table.

❑ Make sure bedding and curtains are at least three feet from electrical outlets.

continued . . .

❏ Cribs should not be positioned on the same wall as an electrical outlet because as the baby grows and the bed level is dropped down, the lowest level for a baby crib is near the exact level as the outlet. Moving the bed later will affect baby's sleeping patterns.

❏ Do not hang mobiles or anything else over the crib that baby can reach and pull down on herself.

❏ Nothing smaller than baby's fist should be within his reach.

❏ Cut any looped curtain or blind cords and make sure they are out of baby's reach.

❏ Put all toxic substances (cleaning supplies, vitamins and minerals, medicines and so on) in high cabinets, even if you have latches on the lower cabinets.

❏ Keep all plants out of baby's reach.

❏ Keep a list of plant names for yourself and your baby-sitter in case baby eats any part of a plant.

❏ Post emergency numbers (including poison control) near ALL phones in the house.

❏ Never leave anything plugged in near a sink, bathtub, toilet or any other source of water.

❏ Consider padding any edges at baby's height (including coffee tables, end tables, sharp chairs and so forth). Use your judgement: some believe baby will learn to be careful around such dangers if they *aren't* padded.

❏ Fasten shelves to walls (so baby can't pull one on top of herself).

❏ Check all toys (new and used) for warning labels, loose parts and broken edges. And be particularly scrutinizing when buying toys at garage sales.

❏ Check all equipment (new and used) for cracks, loose parts, sharp edges, worn joints and a clear mark that the equipment meets national safety standards. Once a car seat has been in an accident, it's unsafe and shouldn't be used again. Also, standards may have changed (as they have for walkers and cribs). If the object doesn't have the manufacturer's name, phone number and the item's model number and date of manufacture, you won't have any way to find out about manufacturer recalls.

❏ Cribs used to have wider spacing between slats and babies used to get their heads stuck before the standards were changed, so using your own crib for your child may be a wonderful thought but a dangerous decision.

❏ If you have a porch, check to be sure it is enclosed by vertical spindles no more than four inches apart. A baby may get caught in—or fall through—anything wider. Don't take a chance!

Feeding and Changing

The most important thing to remember when feeding your baby:

> "Example is not the *main* way to influence others, it is the *only* way."

To peacefully breastfeed or bottlefeed your baby, *you* have to be peaceful. If you want your child to take down a spoonful of soup, try doing it yourself in front of her first so she's not afraid of the spoon. If you want your child to sit at the table and eat with good manners at three to four years of age, the best thing to do is start good table patterning when she's four months old.

Bring the highchair to the table and begin your evening ritual together—even if your baby lasts only five minutes before squirming to get down. You have to plan ahead for dinner and for your child's future behavior now. Eventually, your baby will entertain you every night with grace and good eating habits.

Or, if you'd rather, your child could learn to refuse to eat, refuse to sit down and therefore not be ready for bed on a regular basis. Just picture her, running around like a maniac, screaming "Geronimo!!" as she lands at the bottom of the stairs while you try to entertain guests in the formal dining room.

Remember, it takes time to develop a routine, but a routine is what your baby needs. You have to do it, do it again and do it again until she catches on, and it's far easier to repeat yourself now than to try to break bad habits later.

Stop and smell the roses! Sit down when your baby starts to eat and eat something with her. Smile and make it a fun experience.

1

Breastfeeding Hints

This section is meant to supplement the breastfeeding instructions you receive at the hospital, from your clinic or from a breastfeeding counselor. I will not tell you how to breastfeed; instead I offer a few tips that I hope will help you along the way.

Whether to breastfeed and how long you breastfeed is a personal decision that is yours to make.

Some babies are naturals at breastfeeding and some need to be taught. The same is true for mothers and motherhood.

Do your breasts hear your baby cry and start to leak immediately? Because that's normal.

You have to rotate your baby as much as you have to rotate your breasts because the baby gets cramps.

The more you pump,
the more you make.

If you get a fever, be alert: It
could be the sign of an oncoming
breast infection.

Try to keep your breasts
aired out as much as possible to
avoid infections.

Good old water is the best
remedy I've found for cracked
breasts because some medications
just make it worse.

If you know you will
be converting entirely from
nursing to bottlefeeding on a
certain date, introduce the bottle
only a few days in advance. Babies
catch on remarkably fast. This way,
the only "nipple confusion"
you experience will be
which one to buy.

Still eating for two?

A good friend of mine made a beautiful "dinner home from the hospital" for my husband and me after our first baby was born. I was breastfeeding and starving and I can't even remember all the beautiful foods she prepared. I do remember that later, after breastfeeding my newborn son, he screamed uncontrollably. I was certain he had colic. The next day I learned she had used red pepper and cabbage when preparing the meal for us. From that point on, I decided that macaroni and cheese was just plain easier for everyone.

I've heard that babies who drink smoothly and take long, even swallows you can see in their jaw are likely to sleep through the night sooner.

Bottle Basics

Keep the components of a formula bottle together in one place. Use all the components every time you prepare a bottle. The cap prevents infection and is just as important as the nipple.

Be efficient. Sterilize enough nipples and prepare and pour formula into enough bottles to last 48 hours instead of 24. Presto—You've eliminated half the work!

Sterilize bottle nipples in boiling water for five minutes after each use for baby's first four months.

As store-bought nipples become sticky, replace them. Worn-out nipples keep the baby from drinking smoothly, which will frustrate him.

It's also a good idea to leave new nipples with your baby-sitter, who may not recognize your baby's frustration with worn-out ones.

Did you know that at most stores, you can return or exchange unused diapers that are too small, and baby food and formula that is unopened? Just take them back to the store where you bought them. No questions asked.

Read the directions for mixing formula with water and never deviate from the recipe. Some people try to dilute the formula to get extra or to try to get their baby to lose weight. I've heard of others who try to make it stronger to fill up the baby so he'll sleep. All of these ideas are wrong and very unhealthy for the baby. The measurements for preparing formula should be done exactly as explained on the label.

That's why it's called "formula."

Let your baby eat until she stops. As a rule, try to feed your newborn baby at least 3 ounces at a time. If she does not drink enough, she will be hungry continuously. If she does drink enough, she will sleep better at night.

If your doctor says to feed your baby once every three hours, she means three hours from the *beginning* of the feeding, not the end. For example: If your baby eats her first meal at 7:00 A.M., then you should try feeding her again at 10:00 A.M. and then again at 1:00 P.M. If you count from when she finishes eating, her schedule will always be off and you will be more confused than you are now.

$ Buy formula, diapers and wipes by the case. Your child will use these products for several more months.

Generally speaking, it takes twenty minutes or so to feed your newborn baby, excluding burping.

When feeding your baby before naps or bedtime, try giving her half of what she normally drinks. Then stop, change and burp her (even if it means waking her up). After that, finish the feeding. This way, she won't fall asleep before she is finished eating and she will be more likely to enjoy a longer rest.

If you distinctly smell burning rubber in your house, check to see if a nipple dropped onto the heating element in your dishwasher.

You *can* fool mother nature once in a while! Sucking is instinctive. So if your baby drank a bottle at 10 P.M. and you put her to bed, try feeding her again at 11:30 P.M., even if she is sleeping. If she eats now, you may catch some uninterrupted sleep until 5 A.M. and avoid a middle-of-the-night feeding.

As he grows, your baby will be able to eat more. He will find it easier to sleep longer now. You can put him down to sleep earlier and earlier. Eventually you will be able to enjoy ten to twelve uninterrupted hours if you do it consistently! This should happen at about the four-month mark.

Warm bottles are wonderful. They go down easy, and they put babies right to sleep. But do give a room-temperature or even a cold bottle to your baby every now and then. He will find it strange, but it will prevent a major problem if you are caught unprepared later, when you can't make the bottle "just right" for some reason.

Keep a bib on your baby even when he isn't eating. (Babies spit up at the most unexpected times.) You'll save a mint on clothes.

Although sometimes it seems to take an eternity for a newborn to finish drinking his bottle, believe me, the slower, the better! Infants who drink too fast suffer from unbearable gas.

Remember: gulp = gas.

This is an old wives' tale, but . . . burp your baby after every 3 ounces of liquid. If the baby doesn't burp by the time you count to 300, lay him flat on his back for 60 seconds. Then pick him up and resume burping him while you are standing. (He'll burp then!)

☆ Sanity Tip

Plan a one-day vacation for you and your husband at home. Find a friend and tell her you will gladly reciprocate (someday) but you would like her to baby-sit for the day and evening—at her house. You can go out to lunch or dinner with your husband, clean the house for once, take a nap, stay up late to watch a movie, or just stay home alone and then sleep in.

O nce you give your baby juice, you can kiss those easy, sleep-inducing bottles of warm breast milk or formula goodbye. Babies usually prefer juice once they have tried it.

I f your child refuses to drink anything but juice, give her a serving of formula or expressed breast milk in a colorful "sippy cup" with a lid.

$ Leave tags on all the baby gifts you receive until you use them. Babies grow fast. If you can't use some items (or you have duplicates), you can return them unused for something else you do need. Or the items may make perfect gifts for someone else. (This helps if you are busy and can't get out to shop later.)

Weaning
Ready or not!

Is your baby suddenly hungry all the time? If you are considering feeding your baby oatmeal or rice early, keep in mind that growth spurts don't last very long. Give this stage a week or two and call your doctor before you make any decisions.

The same is true for the reverse of the growth spurt, when baby seems to eat less than usual for a while. And of course, sometimes she is just not hungry. (I wish I were like that!)

If your baby can hold up her head and support her weight while sitting, get the highchair ready: She is probably ready for solid foods!

If you haven't introduced foods by the time your baby is seven months, she is waiting. Remember, one food at a time in case of an allergic reaction.

Weaning tips

- Remember: If you decrease formula or breast milk, your baby is going to get hungry—and that's the key to introducing solid foods.

- Minimize snacks and stick to smaller meals throughout the day, feeding baby in her highchair.

- Finger foods for dipping are excellent small meals.

- Hold off longer in between meals as your baby gets older, until she's on the same eating schedule as you are.

Learning to eat is a stimulating activity that will actually wear your baby out. At about five months old, an hour of eating can equate to a good two hours of sleeping.

Feed your baby when she is hungry. She is growing! (She has the rest of her life to diet.)

R emember, you are also "weaning" yourself from old habits, so keep the following in mind:

- Pack away at least half of your bottles, nipples and accessories so that you don't grab them for convenience.

- Carry more snacks in your diaper bag and leave the house more often for longer periods of time, carrying along only one emergency bottle.

- Tell everyone who cares for your baby what you're doing so that you are all working toward the same goal.

Starter foods

Saltine and graham crackers dissolve easily and are great starter foods. But do not put them in a carry bag or a diaper bag unless they are in a hard container. They will break into a million pieces . . . which is why they are great starter foods!

Beware of the word "never." As in, "I will never take my child to a fast-food restaurant."

Cereals, such as Honeycomb®, and bagels are both excellent starter foods because they taste good and help develop hand-mouth coordination.

Try using a little cup, such as the ones from children's medicine bottles, when helping baby make the transition from bottle to cup. They hold just a little fluid and are fun for the baby to hold—just his size!

The minute they can scoot or crawl, babies head for tablecloths (set for dinner), telephones and electrical cords. Minimize your baby's exposure to these potential hazards! And only use electrical-outlet covers that close automatically.

While he's in the highchair, give your child a plastic, open cup with just a drop of liquid in it. Let him practice using it. Babies learn to drink from a cup amazingly fast. Covered "sippy cups" are great for certain things, but it helps to teach your child the right way the first time.

Vaseline® petroleum jelly is a great barrier cream for your baby's face when you are introducing her to acidic foods, such as oranges and spaghetti sauce. (But be sure to keep it off your clothes.)

If you have a light-colored carpet in your nursery or family room, and you see a busy-print carpet on sale anywhere, buy it and put it over your light carpet to protect it. Leave it there for a few years.

Put a plastic tablecloth underneath the highchair when you feed her. You'll save yourself a lot of needless scrubbing.

⭐ Sanity Tip

For the first year, follow the philosophy that "as long as it gets done" is much more important than "how it gets done" or "who does it." Accept help from anyone, anywhere.

Make eating fun! For instance, when introducing vegetables to your baby, divide them among the separate compartments of a cupcake pan. Not only will your child learn to distinguish one vegetable from another, but it will help you learn which ones he likes best! Just watch him carefully and don't take it personally if he decides to pick up the pan and throw it overboard!

Or, if you don't have a cupcake pan, separate different foods on your baby's plate as much as you can. This way, your child won't accidentally eat something he isn't expecting, especially while he is experimenting with new textures.

I t's likely your child will love to eat meat. Make sure you feed him foods from the other food groups first, such as fruits, vegetables, breads and cereals. Introduce meats last.

I f your baby *doesn't* like meat, get chicken and beef bouillon cubes from the grocery store. They are cheap, so you won't waste a lot of money with this experiment. Add the bouillon cubes to boiling water and then put in alphabet-soup-size pasta. Thicken it to your baby's appropriate spoon-feeding density (meaning more liquid for babies close to one year, less liquid and thicker pasta for younger babies, around six or seven months). Most babies love pasta, so you'll get him used to beef and chicken flavor by filling him up with his beloved pasta. It's slow, but sure.

Instead of feeding your child commercially prepared baby foods at every meal, put a combination of foods from your plate through the blender every now and then. You'll teach your baby to enjoy the same foods your family enjoys.

One of my best friends has a baby who insisted on a Caesar salad with dinner at least once a week after he turned two!

A great way to tell if your baby is aware of the new foods in front of him is to put a finger-size piece of pasta (easy to pick up) next to a cookie. If the baby grabs the cookie first, you'll know he is totally aware of your menu selections. If this happens, you have to keep all cookies, juices and other sweet treats out of his mind until you get him hooked on veggies, fruits, meats and other healthy foods.

If you or your husband are in the grocery store and you've forgotten your shopping list, just buy bread, formula, diapers and pizza.

Babies are not allowed to be born unless they like pizza.

Fussy Eaters

If your child won't try new foods or is a fussy eater, try this:

- Don't feed her too much formula during the day. Formula fills up your baby and makes it that much harder for you to get her to eat something different.

- Try to figure out if it is only "messy" foods—like soup or mashed potatoes—that distress her. Sometimes babies who fuss over their dirty hands and face find soft foods less appealing. You can find out by substituting a new texture, such as dry toast, for the "messy" ones when she's upset.

- Let your baby feed herself if she isn't eating well. She may just want to do it on her own.

continued . . .

- Take her to the food court of your local mall. Seat her next to the salad bar, pasta station or pizza parlor and aim her chair at another baby her age or slightly older who likes what he is eating.

   Your baby loves to learn new tricks to show off, and if you buy her the same food, you will probably see a new side of your baby.

- Try playing a game with her. I like the "beep" game. Say "beep" and, when your baby smiles, try to have her take her first bite. Then only say "beep" after she takes another bite. Babies love games like this, and they figure them out easily.

Fresh air makes for good appetites!

Table Manners

By around one year, your child will walk about and have full reign of the house. Make sure to teach your little one to eat only at the table, because it will save you many hours of cleanup later.

If your child won't eat dinner at the table, try using a candle as a centerpiece and watch what happens!

Flickering candles mesmerize babies as much as they do adults. Just be sure to keep the candle flame far from baby, don't use a tablecloth, and hide all matchbooks.

When your child is five months old or younger and you see her "chewing" instead of sucking, immediately wipe out her mouth with your finger to see if she has anything in there she shouldn't.

Don't let your baby get in the habit of throwing food. If he doesn't eat, he's either not hungry or he doesn't like what you're serving. Either way, make sure you say "no" and then try feeding him the same food again a little later. You can only tell that babies don't like food when you know they are hungry.

Foods with red dye make some children overactive and disruptive. Be wary of foods like ketchup, red juices and red freezer pops.

Make sure your child doesn't play baseball with the potatoes, put carrots in the toilet or broccoli in your drink—at least while your friends are over.

All in the Family

Babies follow the philosophy, "Don't expect me to eat anything that you won't eat."

Don't make your child a pizza for dinner when you are serving chicken to the rest of the family—unless you want her to expect special foods every night.

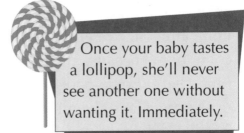

Once your baby tastes a lollipop, she'll never see another one without wanting it. Immediately.

Be advised: Older children will attempt to show your baby by example which foods to eat—and which to avoid. Feed your baby separately if you have older children who won't eat what you want to feed her.

You will continue to receive gifts for baby (think baptism or bris or baby's first birthday). Ask someone in advance to write out or print two or three sets of address labels for your thank-you cards.

D on't wait to instill a love for home in your child. Make family recipes such as "Grandma's secret spaghetti sauce," "Mom's cinnamon rolls," "Dad's pancakes" and "roasted chicken on Sundays." You will be glad you did! Long after they've grown up, your children will come home because they want to taste Mom's (and Dad's) home-cooked meals again.

(Strange fact: Even if they don't eat these family foods right now, they will still learn to love them by smelling them!)

Cut up spaghetti into little pieces and serve small pasta to your baby because they can be a choking hazard until she understands how to maneuver stringy foods. The same applies to melted cheese.

Almost a year!

Children go through "growth spurts" for years. If your child normally picks at food and suddenly seems hungry after every meal, get ready to go shopping! She is probably getting ready to grow again.

I used to tease my sister that my niece "had a hollow leg" because she ate so much as a baby but never gained weight. My first baby was a "picker" and he was huge! Then I had my second child. My second baby eats like a horse but he too gains weight slowly. (Apparently my first one got my genes.) I now realize all babies really are different.

It's hard to stay sane when emotions are running wild, sleep is a memory, people call nonstop and confusion seems to surround you every waking moment. On top of everything, you have just delivered a real baby who looks nothing like all those pictures you've seen in magazines, and you're responsible for her welfare . . . forever. IT IS SCARY, and you deserve a break!

Part of the problem is that during the pregnancy months, we get to relax, we feel good from all of the prenatal vitamins, we rest, we eat well and we learn how to focus and breathe deeply. The minute the baby comes along, however, we forget our basic training. In short, we forget to have a "focal point."

Once you get home from the hospital, your main focal point has to be, "I can do this!"

To help you through this, I'd like to give you a few thoughts you can repeat to yourself any time you feel stressed. I hope they will help you feel better.

Focal Points for New Parents (Repeat to yourself in order up to 100 times daily):

- Smiling is contagious.
- People don't really need eight hours of sleep a day *anyway*.
- Nobody is scoring my parenting skills.
- This is fun and I am really good at this.
- My baby is just begging me for something simple when she cries and I love to help!

Diapers

Does your child eat lots of blueberries? Then don't be surprised to find his diaper has turned blue. (Red juices have a similar effect.) This can be a scary discovery, but don't worry. What goes in must come out!

One of the major signs of dehydration is brick-colored urine—almost red looking. Make sure baby is urinating and that his diaper is wet throughout the day.

Bowel movements look mustardy if baby drinks breast milk and very dark brown if he's on formula.

Onesies

*O*nesies are one-piece undershirts that snap under the bottom. They are great because as your baby grows through the first year, you can put them on under his clothes and they will hold down his shirt and cover his tummy. Babies grow through clothes so fast during this phase that you'll be relieved to know that his tummy won't get cold in a shirt that seems to be shrinking.

Plus, once he starts to pull up his shirt, which can happen anytime when he starts walking, he won't be able to grab at his diaper to pull it off. Babies do this about a year before they even know what the potty is. This signal is not about going to the potty, it's about the plain old fun of pulling things on and off. (Get onesie shirts that snap under the bottom of his diaper and you'll save yourself a lot of wasted diapers.)

I don't think the sizes in children's clothing mean *anything*. For example, my son weighed fourteen pounds at three months, but my nephew weighed nine pounds. Which three-month-old did the tag refer to? Don't miss the joy of seeing your baby in a cute outfit because he outgrew it too fast. Try on everything early and disregard the tags.

If your baby tries to roll over on her tummy whenever you begin to change her diaper, learn to put her diaper on backwards and you'll be set.

Babies grow so fast, you have to file their clothes to keep from going nuts every time you dress them. Keep the bottom dresser drawer empty and use it strictly for clothing that's too small. You will automatically start storing clothes together that are around the same size and avoid hunting through all the drawers for a sweater that fits.

Warm those cold diaper wipes in your hand before you change your baby!

Also, *use* a diaper wipe. The people who say you can save money by not using a wipe at diaper changes are forgetting the additional cost of the doctor visit when the baby gets a rash or fungus.

Don't wake your baby to change a diaper unless she has had a bowel movement and really needs it. (Good diapers are designed to handle these situations and last for hours.)

If an outfit is too big but has feet sewn into it, put it on your baby anyway. Then put a sock over each foot of the outfit.

If the outfit is too small, cut out the feet.

Notice if your newborn baby is starving right after a bowel movement. This will help you identify her schedule and plan.

L et your baby finish his bowel movement before you change his diaper. Unless he has diarrhea, giving him a few minutes will save you a lot more diaper-changing.

Toilet bowls are a hazard too. To protect against drowning, use a toilet-lid lock and keep bathroom doors closed at all times.

Iron

Vitamins with iron can cause constipation in both you and your baby. Use a stool softener yourself and be aware of your baby's bowel-movement schedule for irritability.

Never force anything up your baby's rectum to get him to go, no matter how desperate you get, because the baby will learn to depend on this unhealthy strategy. Just hold his legs up, bent at the knees, and apply pressure to the knees to help push out a bowel movement.

Also, try not to overfeed the baby when he's constipated. Less food may help him feel better and get him to finally go, especially as his body starts getting used to iron. The above also applies if you are using iron-supplemented formula.

Rash decisions

If your baby gets diaper rash frequently, try changing diaper brands. Also, let your baby go diaperless regularly. The longer, the better (at least 10 minutes every waking hour is a tremendous help).

A blistering diaper rash can be the result of a reaction to medicine.

Save yourself a lot of aggravation and keep a set of diapers, wipes and blankets on each level or in each area of your house.

Zinc oxide or Vaseline® petroleum jelly is used on diaper rash. These products create a barrier to protect the baby's skin from his diaper and bowel movements. They also soothe the skin and promote healing. If your child has diaper rash and diarrhea, be sure to use a barrier cream on his bottom—when he's not diaper-free, that is!

☆ Sanity Tip

Mom, if every time you try to lie down and fall asleep, your baby wakes up and you begin to get more tired and frustrated, take a warm shower and pretend to start your day over again.

Have a cup of tea or coffee, and something light to eat to ease the tension. A warm shower usually helps tremendously when you start to feel overwhelmed because it will make you feel like you're being taken care of, too.

One day, one of my best friends came over with her baby, who was about seven months old. He had a big pout on his face and he screamed in a high-pitched tone on and off the entire time they were over. She had taken him to the doctor three days earlier and the doctor had prescribed medicine for an ear infection. She just figured that the high-pitched cry was a symptom of the ear infection.

Well, when she went to change his diaper, I noticed his bottom was *completely red raw* with diaper rash. I mean red like I'd never seen before.

We took off his diaper and dried him off completely. I told her to leave the baby naked because air alone was best for promoting healing. She was panic stricken about having him naked on the car ride home, so I grabbed a pair of toddler underwear from Michael Dean's room and they worked great! Over the next two days, she put them on him now and then when she thought he might have a bowel movement. At night, she still needed to keep the diaper off, so she covered his mattress with a changing pad and a mattress pad on top of that.

But keeping him naked was just the beginning. She needed to know two more things:

1. The rash could be an allergic reaction to the medication. (Bingo! The doctor immediately changed the prescription. She wouldn't have gotten rid of the rash no matter what she did while he was still on that medication.)

2. The symptoms of diaper rash don't go away while you watch them. It's kind of like the old saying: "A watched pot never boils." No matter what you do, you won't see signs of healing until about 24 hours later.

I know it may seem impossible to keep your child "aired out" if he goes to daycare, but don't forget you have weekends—use them to your advantage and keep your baby naked as much as you can. Also, keep him naked when you're home during the week and ask your caregiver to do as much as she can to leave him diaper-free.

Sleeping

Sleeping is the key to a peaceful baby and, just as important, a peaceful home. Figuring out how to get a baby to sleep and get enough sleep may be a bit of a challenge, but think of it as a puzzle with each little piece having a purpose. Try to look at the big picture on the box, rather than the puzzle piece. For example, your baby may not sleep through the night for months, but if you focus on getting him to sleep longer and longer each night, in small increments, you won't be as frustrated.

Two of the most common misconceptions new parents have about sleeping are 1) they believe their baby is different than all the other millions of babies ever born and that their baby simply doesn't need much sleep; and 2) they believe their new baby can climb out of the crib. If you refuse to believe either of these two things, you are well on your way to developing successful sleeping patterns in your child.

Remember, ALL babies and toddlers under three need sleep and lots of rest.

Developing a Routine

Getting a baby to sleep through the night is like testing the deep end of a pool. Prepare yourself mentally and venture a little further each night.

Good news—eventually, you will make it!

Try this: Each night, from now until the baby catches on, plan to put him to bed for the night at 11 P.M.—not 7 P.M. Give him a bath at 10:30 P.M., play together a little and then, after he's been stimulated and fed, put him down to sleep for good. Your goal should be to train baby to sleep the 12 A.M. to 5 A.M. shift first.

Leaving a baby in a car (running or not, locked or unlocked) is considered abuse and may be reported to the Division of Youth and Family Services (DYFS).

If your baby falls asleep in the car, take her out of the car seat as soon as you get home and put her into her own bed. This simple practice will remind baby that she can go back to sleep after being moved. After all, she did it in the womb!

Don't worry: All babies make liars out of their parents, especially when it comes to sleeping. If you say your baby's sleeping schedule out loud, you can bet she will change it on you. So, if things are going well, don't say a word.

Most important, Mom, listen to your own internal "monitor" . . . Mothers know best!

Every now and then, put your baby into the crib before she falls asleep. This will teach her it's OK to go to bed awake and alone. (I just wish my husband had learned this when he was young.)

Where to Sleep?

S trive to put your newborn baby into the crib instead of the bassinet by six weeks of age. (You don't want him to become too used to the bassinet.) By eight weeks, your baby will be ahead of the game for sleeping through the night—and he will love having his own place.

I f you want to avoid having a family bed later, keep your baby in his own bedroom now, even if he wakes up in the middle of the night and you comfort him. Don't get into the habit of bringing your baby into your bed unless you want him to move in with you later on.

If you have two sets of monitors and a large house, put the base of one and the receiver of the other upstairs. Then put the other receiver and base downstairs and turn both monitors on low. Ta dah! I've just installed an intercom system in your home. You're welcome.

Try to get your baby used to sleeping anywhere from an early age. Don't always use the crib or bassinet for his naps. For example, from Day One, let him take every other afternoon nap in the playpen in a busy room (such as the family room) with the TV on.

Sleeping with your baby is dangerous and it only sets up a habit you and your baby will have to break later.

This includes breastfeeding your baby while you're lying down at night. It may seem easier now, but you're setting yourself up for a struggle later. From the first day home, if you breastfeed, sit up while you nurse and then put the baby down into his crib or bassinet.

Night Changing

Always put your baby to bed in pants that are easy to change, in case an unexpected bowel movement comes along. This way, you can minimize her sleep disruption. And yours!

⭐ Sanity Tip

Sleep is not the only thing that relieves sleep deprivation. Resting with your feet up and eating well also do the trick.

As your baby grows through the first year, leave a pair of slip-on platform shoes or a small stepping stool under the crib. You can change your baby's diaper in the middle of the night without even taking her out of the crib. She won't wake up and you won't hurt your back picking her up and putting her down.

Shedding a Little Light on the Subject

Don't turn on lights during night feedings. It may wake your baby.

I think babies can see in the dark because they're used to it.

A night-light in the room may keep your baby from sleeping deeply. Try using a nearby bathroom or hallway light instead while you are checking on your baby. Keep his room dark.

Some Sound Advice

Fact: Babies wear themselves out mentally when they hear background noises, such as people talking or the radio. This means that even if your baby is sleeping in the middle of the family room, he is still wearing himself out. Isn't that great? So, put your baby down for his afternoon naps in a noisier area than his crib and he'll sleep deeper through the night. An added bonus: He'll also learn to sleep through anything.

If you happen to end up with two or three baby monitors, don't return them immediately. Think: living room, master bedroom, kitchen, grandmother's house. Use them all! (This way you avoid having to move them around the house.)

T houghts on
baby monitors:

1

If your monitor is battery-powered, you don't have to plug it in.

2

Make sure you are listening to your child. Sometimes your baby monitor may pick up other people's monitors. (To test the monitor when you are alone, turn on a music box.)

3

Also remember that other people's monitors may pick up yours. Your best bet is to behave with your child as if someone else is listening.

D on't put a monitor next to baby's head or too close to your head. Put it elsewhere in the room. Don't keep the volume too high, because if you do, baby's frequent stirs and yawns are sure to keep you awake.

S ometimes a music box can actually distress a baby or wake her up, especially after a long day. Instead, sing your baby a soft lullaby. Save the music box for times when baby plays in the crib during the day.

Sanity Tip

Forgive yourself if you make a mistake or lose your patience.

I f you want your child to take a light nap, leave the light on and the overhead fan off. If you want your child to take a deep nap, turn the light off and the fan on.

Troubleshooting Tips

Fans

Place a slow-moving fan in baby's room to circulate air. Turn it on each time you put your baby down to sleep. He will become conditioned to sleeping when he hears this noise—handy when you're on vacation or visiting someone else's home. Babies can learn to sleep deeply with background noises. Be sure not to point the fan at the baby.

Every now and then, don't turn on the fan, so your baby will also be able to sleep when a fan isn't available.

If you put your baby down for a nap at someone else's house, try to put the portable crib in the same position it would be at your house (such as facing the bedroom door, window on the left and so on). Put your baby's head in the same place it would be in the crib at home. Then, turn on the fan!

You can't control a lot of what happens around your baby, including noise. One of the most important advantages of leaving on a fan while your baby sleeps is that if the telephone rings, a car alarm goes off or a fire truck goes by, your baby will not wake up.

Fan tips

- Don't point the fan directly at the baby.
- Plug it into an outlet that's operated by the wall switch.
- Condition your baby by using it whenever you put him into his crib.
- Keep at medium so it isn't too loud.
- Don't use heat fans unless you carefully monitor the temperature of the room (babies easily overheat).
- Mount the fan on a sound surface or use a ceiling fan.
- Turn off the fan before baby usually wakes up if you want him to wake up naturally.
- Remember: Fans also keep out other noises, such as the telephone, doorbell, television and so on.
- Use a portable fan you can bring with you when you travel—near or far.

Blankets and bedclothes

If your infant cries every time you put him down, try warming a thin blanket in the dryer first and then put him down on it. He will probably love it and quiet down immediately.

Remember this trick when you are moving your baby from the bassinet into his crib, and if you want your baby to take a nap when you are visiting friends.

Placing a blanket around your baby in the crib will make him feel more secure and comfortable. Roll up the blanket and encircle your baby closely with it, especially when he is a newborn.

Or, instead of a using a blanket, make the room a little warmer and then dress him very lightly (in a "onesie," perhaps).

Do not use a pillow, puffy comforter or lamb's-wool mattress cover in your baby's crib until she is old enough to lift her head and hold it up. Studies prove that these items contribute to sudden infant death syndrome, or SIDS. Also, try putting your baby down to sleep on her back. If your baby objects, discuss it with your doctor.

First impressions are lasting impressions, even with babies. They become attached to things like blankets and you can't just substitute a blanket later, even if it's identical. They know the difference.

If you're going to allow a blanket and want to prevent dragging along a "dirty-looking-rag blanket" everywhere you go, buy two or three of the same blankets and alternate using them from Day One.

Baths

Bathing an infant before bed calms him. Feed him a warm bottle or nurse him after each bath and he may actually sleep longer.

Use a plastic pasta strainer from the kitchen to store bath toys after use. Take the baby out and throw the toys in the strainer. They'll drain quickly and you'll be set.

Adjust your water heater to a maximum of 120°F or 49°C. That way, you can't accidentally scald your baby with the bath or tap water.

If you run out of traditional baby bubble bath, use a tiny drop of antimicrobial dishwashing liquid and your baby will not only be clean, he'll probably have more bubbles than ever!

Drinking problems?

Don't be surprised if your baby is thirsty after her bath. She's probably dehydrated, which is easy to fix. It's no different than when you feel thirsty after swimming in a pool or sitting in a hot tub. Don't worry about giving her too much liquid after a bath, especially before bedtime. If you *don't* give your thirsty baby a drink before bed, you can be sure you will have to get up to give her a drink later!

☆ Sanity Tip

Make a large "Do Not Disturb" sign for your front door. And don't forget to use it whenever you need to!

Don't give your child juice in the middle of the night. Besides not being good for her teeth, juice is mostly sugar and will wake her up.

On the flip side, if she is grouchy and needs a long time to wake up, give your baby a little bit of orange juice in the morning. The orange juice will also help prevent colds.

The best medicine

Babies laugh when they're tickled. They laugh even more when you laugh. And they sleep best after they laugh.

Over-the-counter pain medicines for teething, fevers and so on are available in four-hour and eight-hour doses. With your doctor's approval, use the eight-hour ones so baby can get a good night's sleep without the medication wearing off.

If your baby has a cold or continually has a crusty nose even when he's not sick, use a vaporizer in his bedroom at night to moisten the air and help him sleep better.

If your baby wakes up in the night screaming, but does not open her eyes (as though she were still asleep), she may have a gas bubble. Try burping her or using a gas-relief product first. Don't immediately try to feed the baby; it could make her more miserable. And it may reverse all the progress you made in weaning her from night feedings.

$ Trade in or sell your maternity and outgrown baby clothes at a second-hand clothing shop.

By three months old, your baby should be able to physically handle not eating during the night. The problem is that she is used to being fed on demand, so first you have to concentrate on dropping the feeding, not on sleeping through the night. The way to do this is to not only stop the night feedings completely, but also change the way you feed her during the day—don't jump up to feed her the moment she cries. She'll expect the same at night. Soon she'll adjust to the routine of not eating at night. It takes a good week to learn, although some would call it a "bad week"!

Ingredients for a Good Night's Sleep

- Fresh air before bed
- Activity twenty to forty minutes before bed, unless your baby is overstressed
- Love, softness and calmness during bedtime feeding
- New diaper
- Bath
- Fan while she sleeps
- Baby must be fed or she sleeps lighter and wakes up easily because she's hungry. Feed your baby within fifteen minutes of bedtime. After five months, use thicker foods to fill her up, such as soup with crackers, or pasta or toast.

*"*If it ain't broke, don't fix it." If baby is sleeping well and acting happy, don't change a single thing!

Checking on Baby

Check baby at bedtime. Roll back his sleeves if they might cover his hands in the night. This way, he won't wake up later because he cannot get to his thumb or hand to soothe himself.

Let your newborn baby sleep! It depends on the baby of course, but more likely than not, your baby can sleep all day at this age and then sleep just as well at night. Check on him regularly, and I say, if he's OK, you're OK!

☆ Sanity Tip

Sleep when your baby sleeps.

As your baby grows, it gets harder to hear him cry, not easier, so if you're going to let your baby cry for intervals to get him to sleep through the night, do it between months three and four and you'll be set.

If you baby's not sleeping from 7 P.M. to 7 A.M. (or 8 P.M to 8 A.M.) by the time he's taking two longer naps each day, he's running behind.

Start putting him down for a morning nap from about 9 to 11 and an afternoon nap from about 1 to 3. Remember: Dozing is always OK, and welcome, but sleeping deeply after 3 P.M. kills the night schedule.

If you are letting your baby cry in the crib and he is almost quiet, don't let him see you checking on him. The minute he sees you, you'll be back to square one!

Is your baby a light sleeper? You will need to teach him that just because he wakes up rarin' to go whenever someone goes by, it doesn't mean that person intends to pick him up and take him out for a walk.

Believe it or not, one of the main reasons that babies (and their parents) don't sleep well at night is that they are overtired! How bizarre is that? Keep yourself and your baby from being overtired by taking regular naps. Your baby will sleep better at night.

Your baby will perform random "mom checks." If he checks for you in the middle of the night, let him know you are near by patting his back, but avoid picking him up. (If you pick him up, he will remember his great success and try it again every night thereafter.)

Baby will probably try to make her way around the crib as she gets older. Tuck in her blanket at the foot of the crib so she won't become tangled in it as she crawls forward.

If your child wakes up and wants to play with you at 1 A.M., don't do it! Teach your baby that if she wants to stay up alone, it's up to her—but you plan to get some sleep. Monitor her closely, but don't respond unless you are prepared to play with her every night at that time.

Don't worry, Mom—it takes nine months to put on the pounds, so give yourself *at least* nine months to take them off. Drink lots of water and you'll be fine.

Don't take your child for car rides to get her to sleep. It is a dangerous practice and it develops bad habits. If this is how you get your baby to sleep, you might as well start a taxi service, because now you will have to drive your wonderful baby someplace every time you want her to sleep.

The Golden Rule of sleeping through the night is this: If you turn on the TV or entertain your baby late at night even once, your baby will expect you to entertain her every night at that same time.

When your baby is around six months old and learns how to stand up in the crib, he may start crying—more out of fear that he doesn't know how to let go and sit back down than because he wants you to take him out. Rather than pick him up, because this will just form a new bad habit, bend his knees, show him how to sit back down, pat his back, say "I love you" and leave the room immediately.

Your baby has guardian angels and smiles at them all the time. Have you noticed?

Once your child learns to say, "But I'm not tired," say, "What does that have to do with anything? Good night!"

Naps

Whenever I think of cat naps, I think of my grandfather—on a hammock on the front porch or in a glider swing. Wherever I found him, he was always napping peacefully!

If your baby likes cat naps too—dozing off here and there instead of sleeping deeply—give him lots of fresh air. Try using a portable swing (they even come in a glider style).

Sometimes your baby will be so tired that you'll have to close his eyes for him.

If your baby is running on schedule, but won't take a nap, let her play naked for fifteen minutes. That airs her out and makes her feel good. Afterward, dress her snugly, give her a warm bottle and try the nap again.

If your baby will not take a nap, make her spend at least 1-1/2 hours each day in a quiet room. Babies and mothers need rest and "down time" to be pleasant.

Waking Up

The best way to wake up your baby so he won't be grouchy is to turn off the fan or gently open the blinds about fifteen minutes before you want to get going. (By the way, closing the blinds while baby is sleeping may help him sleep better, too.)

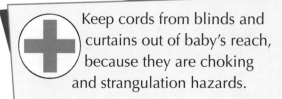 Keep cords from blinds and curtains out of baby's reach, because they are choking and strangulation hazards.

Ways to keep a baby awake:

- Change his activity.
- Give him a different toy to play with.
- Change how he's situated: For example, move him from bouncing seat to jumper.
- Visit a friend.
- Go to the grocery store or the post office.
- Sing a song.
- Give the baby a dab of orange juice (if he is older than five months).

New babies often sleep when there are noises going on around them, especially sounds they do not recognize. It's almost like they're hiding from them. When it's absolutely quiet and your baby thinks the coast is clear, don't be surprised if she opens her eyes and even starts to coo.

Keep this in mind because making things perfectly silent can actually wake your baby up peacefully from a nap.

Once your baby establishes a morning wake-up schedule, she will probably be more reliable than your alarm clock.

I used to think that the worst thing about vacationing was trying to get the baby to sleep through the night in a new place. This bothered me to the point that just the fear of it kept us from spending much quality time at the beach together as a family.

But, I figured it out!

The way to save a vacation is to outlast your baby on the first attempt to get him to sleep, no matter how long it takes. Then he gets used to the new sleeping area and it becomes his routine for the rest of the trip.

My babies were complete opposites. Michael Dean was born in the summer and was used to sleeping almost anywhere, anytime. Even so, the first vacations were tricky for me. Brandon was born during the coldest, snowiest winter that I can remember. Unless someone locked me out of the house, he slept in his crib or in the family room in his playpen, especially at night.

Well, I was terrified, but when Brandon was eight months old, we went on vacation in Florida. We stayed in an RV park and the only place that Brandon could sleep was on a bunk bed with a guard rail. (Yeah, right.) I wasn't really sure what he'd do about having to sleep in a new place. He was a private boy and he liked to sleep in his cozy little crib.

Well, first I lay down with him and tried to get him to rest, but he wasn't used to me being with him, so he was cranky and then he was preoccupied with the railing, windows, and this fun new area.

Normally, at this time of day, Brandon would be sound asleep, but he was acting wide awake and it was obvious that this was going to be a long process. If I wanted to have a good vacation, I would have to outlast him the first time in order to get him to sleep the rest of the nights and naps.

We went through crying and reading and playing and trying to get down and, finally, screaming, but I stayed calm and didn't give up.

For two long hours.

Finally, after another ten minutes, he purred like a kitten in my arms and slept. After that, he knew that area was where he was going to sleep and he knew that it didn't matter how long he fussed—he wasn't getting down.

So after that first struggle, he went to sleep in his new place right away. From the get-go our trip was perfect. If I had given up, he would have known that he could outlast me, and then every night and naptime afterward would have been complete chaos.

Now, I use this same process everywhere we go. My mother always says, "Parenting is a test of two wills. Yours versus your baby's." The first time you try something is usually the hardest, but it's the most important time because it sets the rules. Remember: Babies beg for boundaries. They want you to win so they know what to do.

Health

Baby's health should be your number-one priority. Everything you do now will affect your baby throughout her life, so please make sure she gets her immunizations, do what you can to introduce her to all types of food early and keep your baby in hazard-free areas.

Also, keep in mind that you can't always protect your baby from things like catching a cold or the flu. In fact, sometimes when babies are exposed early to other sick children, perhaps at daycare, they pick up minor infections that actually kick their immune systems into overdrive, resulting in fewer sicknesses as they grow. Go figure!

Healthy is from the inside out, so don't forget to instill a positive, productive value system in your baby early. Once they start using their "memory bank" to solve problems, they never stop.

Some Common Concerns

Aches and pains

Growing pains are a real medical condition. Bone grows faster than muscle, which causes an aching pain. It's common for children between three and six to complain about this, so can you imagine how a new baby must feel? Maybe that's why so many people recommend baby massages.

This is an old wives' tale, but I've heard that when your baby hiccups, he's about to grow.

Allergies

Your baby can become allergic to anything (for example, diapers and formula), even if he has used or eaten the same items before without a reaction. Babies may react to a change in laundry detergents, too.

Bad breath

As a general rule, new babies should never have bad breath. If your newborn does, take her to a pediatrician because it could be a sign of infection in the mouth or somewhere else in the body.

If you want to experience something wholly natural, watch the way your child climbs stairs.

Cuts and scratches

Use a tiny dab of diaper cream on your baby's cut or scratch because the ointment's purpose is to promote healing—and don't forget to use it on your own cuts and scratches, too!

Ears and nose

I f baby's nose is stuffy, he will be unable to drink or sleep soundly. Check with his doctor. Use a vaporizer in his room and hold him up in a sitting position while he is trying to drink.

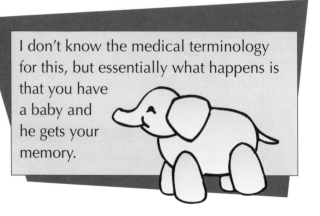

I don't know the medical terminology for this, but essentially what happens is that you have a baby and he gets your memory.

I f your baby is stuffed up and you don't have a vaporizer, take him into the bathroom, close the door and run the shower until the bathroom steams up. Stay there with your baby for up to twelve minutes at a time. Do this as often as you can while he is sick—at least once every two hours.

Of course, it really is much easier to just get a vaporizer for twenty bucks and put it in his bedroom on a hard surface. It is truly a baby essential.

Every home with a baby should have two infant bulb syringes . . . one for noses and one for ears. They are made differently and have different uses. The nose syringe is especially helpful because you can clear a baby's nose with it just before feeding. He'll drink better, especially when he is sick.

Don't let Junior near other children if he's sick or has been sick in the past twenty-four hours (even if he seems fine). It's not fair to the other children—or their parents!

Ear problems in babies are frequently caused when fluid builds up in the ear and it becomes infected.

No one ever wants to admit that cotton-tipped applicators are really made for the nose. But if my sister (a nurse) hadn't shown me how to use one to clean my son's nose, he'd still be walking around with dried boogers caked on. Now, I keep cotton-tipped applicators in my purse, car, diaper bag and my husband's briefcase. Sometimes, it's the only way to get those out-of-reach crusties. Just be gentle.

Fever

You may be able to tell if your child has a fever just by holding her next to you. If your baby feels different, especially if she feels hot, use a thermometer to see if she has a temperature.

☆ Sanity Tip

Forgive yourself if you don't diagnose or notice something important about your baby. You are a mother, not a rocket scientist. (And if you are a rocket scientist, you are probably still not a pediatrician, psychologist, teacher, speech pathologist and pharmacist. And if you are, then you probably already knew the answer anyway, so why are you asking me?

The expert about your child is not your doctor. It's you!

Gagging

Don't panic if your child seems to be gagging on something. Give him a second to "cough it up" reflexively. (If your husband is panicking, gag *him*.)

Hyperactivity

If your child is wound up and imitates the Tasmanian Devil, try removing all sugar from his diet before you have him examined for attention deficit disorder (ADD).

Some juices have lots of sugar, so avoid them. Watch liquids such as iced tea, apple juice and powdered drinks, too.

Teething

Around the eigth month, babies begin to chew a lot because their teeth are starting to come in.

Chilled teething rings and biter biscuits come in handy. Two other great ideas are chilled oat rings and chilled fruit from a baby-food jar. Things that are hard help the teeth come through the gums and colder foods may be more comfortable for baby to eat during this time. Give her something to bite and teething will soon be a thing of the past . . . just make sure it's not your nose!

Some doctors will never agree that your baby is teething, but mothers know better! And don't be surprised if you never hear a peep from your teething child. Some babies just don't mind teething.

Keep a brightly colored dishtowel in the freezer. It makes a great homemade toy—babies are fascinated with colorful towels—and the coolness will soothe her gums when she sucks on the towel.

Home Care

If your child falls down, don't assume he hurt himself. Check him over right away, but remember: Your reaction may have a greater effect on your baby than the accident itself.

Babies are generally terrified to see their body produce anything other than sounds. This is true for vomiting, bowel movements and so on. Always remember to stay calm if your baby is disturbed. Again: Your reaction is going to set the stage for his reaction.

When your child shows you his "boo-boo," he is baring his soul. Always acknowledge him.

Don't forget the chicken soup if your child is sick. Thicken soup by adding broken crackers to the broth.

Trust your instincts!

If your child has a stomach virus, stick to fluids like flat ginger ale and white grape juice, in case she needs to vomit. I can say from experience that crib sheets and walls will be ruined if your child drinks anything red, orange or purple.

★Sanity Tip

Limit yourself to doing laundry one day a week—otherwise you will go crazy.

Try filing baby's nails instead of cutting them, especially if your personal style is more like a bull in a china shop than like a ballerina.

It is easier to file or cut nails when babies are sleeping.

Always empty water pails as soon as you are done with them. Babies can easily fall into water pails.

☆Sanity Tip

Don't be distressed if you notice your six-month-old baby is wearing you out more than ever. You've been through six months of hormonal changes. In the meantime, your baby has enjoyed lots of sleep, a good diet and plenty of exercise. He's probably ready for the Junior Olympics!

Medicine

When using a dropper for baby medicine, place the end of the dropper under the baby's tongue and dispense the medicine. If you try to dispense the medicine on top of her tongue, she will spit it out.

If you are trying to give your baby medicine, use a nipple! Babies will suck the medicine from a nipple as though it were breast milk or formula, without knowing the difference.

Don't hesitate to buy low-cost alternatives for some baby items, especially medicines. Often they are made by the same manufacturer and are exactly the same product as the higher-priced advertised brand.

Keep a bottle of ipecac syrup on hand. Ipecac syrup induces vomiting. Be aware that some things babies swallow shouldn't be vomited, but treated another way. At your baby's next appointment, talk to your doctor about the situations for which ipecac may be advised.

Remember the poor man's medicine and give your child lots of water.

Over-the-counter pain-relief medications can mask your child's illness. They temporarily take away the symptoms without curing the underlying sickness. Don't use these products without checking with your doctor first.

If your child indicates he actually wants to take medicine, move all of it to another place and double-lock the cupboard doors. This includes vitamins and the aspirin or other medications you might carry in your purse.

If your child is sick and does not sleep, he may be over-medicated. (Some decongestants contain antihistamines or are high in sugar.) Also, observe your child for any other reaction to medicine.

If you find yourself at the doctor's office constantly, perhaps because your baby gets ear infections or sinus problems, ask your doctor to treat your baby with a different medicine.

Often the doctor has several options to choose from, so if one medicine isn't working, you can try another. Your baby will appreciate your looking into this for him and discussing it with your doctor.

Going to the Doctor

Before calling your doctor's office with a concern about your baby, be sure you know baby's temperature. Your doctor will ask about this right away. Doctors usually prefer a rectal reading.

Well-baby checkups are done at

2 weeks	9 months
1 month	12 months
2 months	15 months
4 months	18 months
6 months	24 months

and at each birthday that follows, until your doctor says you are excused.

If your baby is due for a shot, try giving him his favorite toy about two minutes before the nurse gives the shot. Take it away just before the shot, and your baby will look to you for the toy. After the shot, when the baby starts to wail, smile and say, "I'm sorry, honey," and give him back the toy. He will probably forget about the shot as soon as he gets his toy back. (And let me tell you, if a baby can forget about a shot that easily, he'll also forget that you had anything to do with it.)

Videotape your baby if he does something unusual you want his doctor to see, because children never do what you want them to do when you want them to do it. (Videotape your child regularly anyway. In the event he is lost or missing, videos show more distinguishing characteristics than photos do. Police stations sometimes offer videotaping services for your child.)

Try to schedule your baby's doctor's appointment as the first one of the day or the first one back from lunch hour so you won't have to wait in line at the appointments desk. Also, to save time, call the office a half hour before your appointment to see if the doctor is on schedule.

Bear in mind that, although the file in the doctor's office may contain almost a year's worth of information, you are the one in charge of noticing repeat occurrences and reporting them—not the other way around.

Keep your child's health records up to date in a file, notebook or large manila envelope that stays in the same place, a particular drawer or shelf. Bring the file to doctor's appointments for instant updating. Added bonus: If you keep records yourself, you'll always have them when you need them—especially at times when the doctor's office is closed, such as on weekends.

Special concerns

If you feel your child may have a learning disability, don't wait. Take your child to a specialist. Most parents of children with disabilities say they "had a feeling" long before it was confirmed.

Burn Watch: Once your baby starts to crawl, be sure she doesn't try to stand up by pulling on the stove (such as the oven door). Watch that she doesn't reach up to touch one of the heating elements or pull a pot off the stove. Don't let your baby play on or around your stove at all!

This goes for irons and ironing boards, too. Always put them away when you are done.

If your child squints, have her eyes checked. If she only reacts to the TV if the volume is high, have her ears checked.

Testing babies is difficult; it's probably best to assume results are questionable to the age of four, when children are easier to test. If you are suspicious about the results or notice ongoing symptoms, get a second opinion.

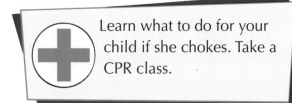

Learn what to do for your child if she chokes. Take a CPR class.

If your child isn't doing something another child her age is, don't panic. Write yourself a note and check it out at your next doctor visit. Your child may be doing something already that the other child isn't. Don't worry unless the doctor says to.

By the time my baby was six months old, he had been sleeping through the night for about two months. I knew his routine inside out. Then one night, I heard a strange noise on the monitor, strange enough that I rushed into his bedroom (something I don't usually do when I hear the typical noises).

Anyway, I looked into the crib and saw vomit all over everything. I immediately picked him up and when I started to give him a hug, he puked again . . . all over me. It wasn't a pretty sight. At this point, he was wide awake and I was not only worried about what was making him throw up, I realized that he was going to be wide awake for a *long* time: He'd gone to bed at 7:00 P.M. and now it was about 1:00 A.M.—he'd already slept about six hours. The only thing I could do was replace and wash all the sheets, give him a bath and, while I was at it, get into the bathtub with him.

Well, after a few minutes in the tub, he was happy as a lark, playing with his rubber ducky. I was still terrified because I had a meeting first thing the next morning.

We got out of the bath and he acted fine. He had no temperature and although he may have been able to drink a bottle, I was afraid the formula would only make him feel more sick because his puke had looked like formula. (In fact, formula that's been exposed to air for too long can make a baby throw up. Read the container. When in doubt, throw it out!)

I didn't have a clue what to do so I called my sister, who conveniently worked the night shift on the maternity floor at our local hospital. I remember saying,

"Hi, Julie, it's now 2:30 in the morning and I have a wide-awake baby who might be sick because he threw up all over twice. What do I do?"

And she said that doctors often recommend diluted chamomile tea for colicky babies older than two weeks, because it calms their tummies. It's also a good remedy for children and babies under one who throw up. I grabbed a chamomile tea bag, made a cup of tea for myself, took the same tea bag and used it again in an 8-ounce bottle and gave it to Brandon.

And, he actually drank some of it (which I didn't expect and thought was weird)! The next thing I knew, we were both back to bed, sound asleep.

The next night, I searched the internet and learned that chamomile tea is recommended exactly as she described and also that many foreign countries traditionally give babies chamomile tea in the last bottle of the day. Not only does it mellow out the baby and help him sleep better, it also helps wean him from bottles because the tea always makes him too tired to drink the whole bottle.

What a great ritual!

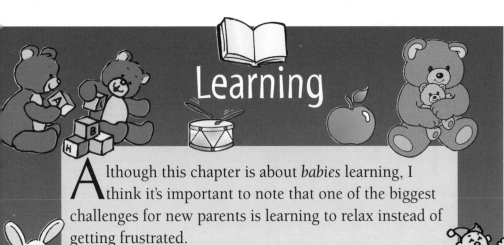

Learning

Although this chapter is about *babies* learning, I think it's important to note that one of the biggest challenges for new parents is learning to relax instead of getting frustrated.

It's a fact that adults are used to their own routine and control over situations. Basically, when a new baby comes along, chaos occurs. Remember, babies are born with their own will and free spirit and this is a remarkable gift. We are all individuals and our uniqueness makes us great.

Learn to smile, sit back and ride the wave of your child's personality instead of going against it. The way to do this is to let your baby be himself. To have a content baby, you have to learn his personality and then provide him with toys and activities that support his natural qualities. If you have a busy child, give him toys with lots of buttons, bells and whistles. If your child is quiet, give him lots of books, mirrors and mellow things. If your child is cranky, give him less stimulation during these times and make sure you stick with juices that are made with natural sugar, such as orange juice, rather than anything else (throughout his life, by the way).

Also, try not to label your baby because he understands from birth how you feel about him and he hears you when you talk about him. As an example, consider a toy "challenging," and your child "perfect in every way." If anyone calls your child "spirited," consider it a great compliment and thank them!

Schedules

There are two schedules to think about: One is baby's natural schedule and the other is the family's real life schedule. It's your job as a parent to get them both to work together.

From the very first day, children keep their own schedules. They do some things the same way, every day—such as bowel movements. Watch for the schedule and you will learn to relax. And if you help keep your child on her schedule, she will be more content.

Consider the expression "adjustment period" to mean the time baby needs to get accustomed to your family's schedule, not the time your family needs to adjust to her schedule.

To learn your child's schedule, log his activities and bowel movements in a notebook or a personal computer over a twenty-four-hour period. Add information to your notebook every day. Fill in some details, too, such as when he is alert or quiet. Post the schedule on your refrigerator and give your baby-sitter a copy.

Children become their parents, so do what you can now to help them become great parents later.

If the clock has changed because of daylight-saving time, the baby's schedule will change temporarily, too.

If you still can't find a schedule in your baby's day, create one! Start with meals served at the same time every day. Then add naps, bedtime and playtime . . . in that order. If you get your baby onto some type of schedule right away, you will be like the efficient beaver building her dam, rather than like the gardener who was so busy trimming bushes, she didn't have time to sharpen her scissors.

Sample schedules

When my son Michael Dean was born, we tried to stick to a schedule wherever we went. We didn't have to be at home because the schedule could be adjusted to fit any situation. For example, if he fell asleep in the car, he'd still have his regular nap time: he'd just rest and learn to play in his crib. If the schedule got completely thrown off, we'd just pick it up again once we got home and back into our routine. Usually, though, you can keep a simple schedule even when you're on vacation.

The following pages include sample schedules based on Michael Dean's first years. If you're having trouble getting a schedule started with your baby, try using these samples as a starting point and adjust them to fit your lifestyle.

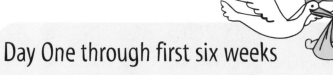

Day One through first six weeks

- I changed his diaper whenever it needed it and let him sleep whenever he wanted to.

- I kept his bassinet in a corner of the family room during the day and moved it into our bedroom at night. Michael Dean also had his own crib in his own bedroom. My goal was to get him into the crib during the nighttime hours as soon as possible (by eight weeks at the latest).

- His schedule naturally fell into two-hour increments for feeding. Sometimes he slept ten minutes, other times longer. During the day, I fed him every two hours by the clock, beginning at 5:10 A.M. no matter what. By six weeks, I'd let him sleep as long as he could between 12:10 A.M. and 5:10 A.M. My only rule was that I wouldn't feed him more than once in a two-hour period, except if it meant feeding at 4:00 A.M. and getting back on track at 5:10 A.M.

From around six weeks to around four months

A.M.

7:00   **Wake up**

7:10   **Breastfeed**

7:45   **One-on-one play:** Smiling practice!

8:15   **Crib time:** Put him in his crib awake to keep him acquainted with it. I had a mobile and toys hooked on the side for him to view.

8:30   **Upright play, bath or errands:** Move him into a more upright position and either play with him on the floor or put him in his bouncing seat or swing with a new activity. Or give him a bath, depending on his mood. (This morning period was noisy, so if I had to run errands, this was the time to do it. These, of course, would take longer than fifteen minutes and if they did, I'd feed him at 9:10 no matter where we were.

8:45   **Playpen time:** If home I'd put him in his carrier seat inside his playpen to introduce him to it. (If it didn't work, I'd just try again next time. Of course, if he dozed off, I was thrilled!)

9:10   **Breastfeed**: two hours from the *start* of the last feeding

9:45   **Naptime:** Put him down in his crib to train for a longer morning nap. (This was in a quiet, dark room with a fan running. The goal of this period of time was to work toward a consistent nap in the morning. By this point, he had eaten twice, probably bathed and had been stimulated in a busy area, especially if we went outside in the fresh air to play or run errands.

11:10   **Feed**: At this point, I used a bottle because I wanted to use both.

11:40   **Free play or nap** for about an hour and a half in an open place. (If I had any place to go, or if I wanted to visit someone, this was another time I would do it.)

continued . . .

From around six weeks to around four months (continued)

P.M.

1:10   **Feed:** At this stage, feeding every two to three hours worked great.

1:40   **Naptime:** Again, I was working toward a goal of a predictable nap. This time, I used the portable fan downstairs and let the baby sleep in the playpen or the bassinet.

3:10   **Feed**

3:40   **Free play or nap:** Again, I was going for about two hours of activity or napping in an open, busy area. Outside activities and fresh air were perfect at this time.

5:10   **Feed**

5:40   **Cranky hour/dinnertime:** In the beginning, this was Michael Dean's "stress-out time" or "cranky hour," and it was also about the time my husband walked in starving, so I had to be creative. My first choice would be to put the baby in the swing in the kitchen and pray that he would relax and drift off to a light sleep, but if he was overloaded, the swing made him more irritable and that was the signal to move upstairs to the quiet crib area until after we all ate a peaceful dinner. I had two goals: 1) Don't overstimulate Michael Dean during cranky hour, and

2) keep my marriage happy. After about thirty to forty-five minutes, we would bring the baby downstairs (even if we had to routinely wake him up) and, usually, put him on a blanket on the floor and just lie with him and have family time for the next hour or so.

7:10	**Feed**

7:40 **Play or naptime:** For the next couple hours, allow him to doze off here and there in the swing or playpen or bassinet, in the same room with us. (I didn't put the baby in a quiet room again until bedtime, around 11:00 or 12:00. Stimulation during this time would help him sleep better later.)

9:10 **Feed**

9:40 **Play**

11:10 **Feed**

11:30 **Quick bath, quick body massage, rock the baby quietly.**

12:00 (A.M.) **Feed before bed:** At the latest, I would feed the baby a small amount at around midnight to fill him up and then I'd burp him and put him to bed and he started sleeping until around 7:00 A.M.

Note: Feeding often during the day helped him eat less at night. Keeping him stimulated during the day with fresh air and then putting him to bed later at first helped him sleep from 12:00 to 5:00, then soon from 12:00 to 7:00.

Somewhere around four months through his second birthday

A.M.

7:00   **Wake up**

7:10   **Breastfeed** (or breakfast after weaning)

7:30   **Playtime**

8:30   **Feed in the highchair**:
        By six months, this
        took up to an hour because I introduced
        foods that he could try to pick up by
        himself to practice coordination. This
        became his morning activity and it wore
        him out and filled him up. It also allowed
        me to get a lot of things done.

9:30   **Naptime** (in his crib)

11:30   **Feed then playtime**: about two hours of
        activity or napping in an open, busy area,
        including more highchair training and
        my favorite class, "Introduction to New
        Foods 101."

P.M.

1:00   **Feed then naptime in playpen.**

3:00   **Feed** (in high chair) **then playtime:**
Again, about two hours of activity or
dozing in an open, busy area worked best.
Outside activities and fresh air were
perfect at this time of day.

5:30   **Feed then bathtime:** I fed him the
heaviest foods of the day to help him
begin to wind down. It was hard, but I
would try to keep him awake because he
hadn't done anything except doze since he
woke up at around 3:00 P.M.
This was a perfect time to
give him a bath because it
not only wore him out, it
kept him awake.

7:00   **Feed, short body massage, bedtime in
the crib.** (From five months to a year, I
would try to feed him food first and then
fill him up with the bottle or breast
after—not before.)

Changing baby's routine

Look for "loopholes" in your baby's pattern—and take advantage of them. For instance, if one night your child is exhausted but awake, put her to sleep without a bottle. If she goes to sleep, try to omit the bottle from the ritual the next night also.

Try to break baby's bad habits while you're in a new environment. For example, "lose" a bottle or a pacifier while you are on vacation. In new surroundings, baby may become preoccupied and forget that item more easily than she would at home.

Sanity Tip

Around the time I had just had my first baby, Michael Dean, I depended on a ritual: Every morning, afternoon and evening (or so), I would microwave some water to make a cup of instant coffee or soothing tea. Then one day, in the very beginning when I needed it most, my microwave died and I couldn't afford a new one. I went without anything for days, dragging around in a fog.

Finally, my mother called me and said, "Why don't you just boil a cup of water on the stove?" and it was like my eyes were opened to a whole new world.

Discipline

S omeone once said, "There is no love without discipline, and there is no discipline without love," and I agree completely.

N o matter what, mother and father must show a united front where baby is concerned.

Parenting reminds me of the fashion industry. The leaders set the trends, but the tried and true are always in style.

D on't ever laugh at your child's bad habits. Stop them right away!

For instance, if your baby tries to get his way by throwing a temper tantrum, take away the toy he's playing with or adjust the situation so you're in control. He will learn what you say, goes. The longer you wait, the harder it will be to change his behavior.

Don't be afraid to say "no" to your baby, and start early.

Sometimes you just have to fake out your children. For example, if you want them to sit by the window, put them by the door instead. They will head for the window automatically!

Don't try to reinvent the wheel. If you have friends who are mothers, take their advice. It saves a lot of time and upset.

When you can look deep into your child's eyes and know he knows exactly what he is doing, it's time to start setting rules.

*V*eteran mothers have learned that you check on babies when you *don't* hear them, less often when you do.

Isn't it wonderful—when your baby is about to walk, many people will advise you to remove sharp-sided furniture, such as the coffee table, from your home. They say your child might hit his head on it if he loses his balance standing up those first wobbly times. Bumping his head could make him hesitate to try standing and walking again. For a little while!

However, just as many people will tell you to leave your furniture right where it is and let the baby get used to it. If you do leave your furniture in place, pad the sharp corners just to be safe.

Don't let your child run the family. The father is the father, the mother is the mother, and the child is the child. And that's OK!

The sounds of an ambulance, fire truck and police car take on new meaning once you are a parent, don't they?

Infants are born secure and then develop insecurities. Say "You are not allowed to because I said so," and "That is too dangerous to play with," instead of "You can't do that."

Parenting as Teaching

A child doesn't really "hate" anything. Things like the crib or the bouncing seat may just frighten her at first because she is unsure of it. Teach your baby to enjoy these things by introducing them at a slow, comfortable pace.

Try putting your baby into a bouncing seat or car seat at an early age. Place the seat inside her playpen for a few minutes now and then. She will get used to the playpen this way. By the time she is ready for it, your baby will love spending lots of time playing in her "special" place.

Traditions are an important kind of "routine." Build a tradition with your child. For instance, my mother gives my children and their cousins the same Easter bunny every year to play with for a week. You should see their faces light up when they see their old friend!

If your newborn isn't used to the swing yet, don't give up! Try again—and again! Babies change every day.

If you are an uptight parent, you probably have an uptight baby. If this is true for you, take ten deep breaths and remember to smile at your baby every time you look at him.

Have you ever noticed it's always the parents who say they have bad kids who actually do? Don't call your child names or tell him he is "bad" unless you *want* him to be, because he hears and believes everything you say.

B abies get bored quickly, but there is an up side: For example, you can use the swing for fifteen minutes and then use it again fifteen minutes later and baby will think it's a new activity!

T each your child to be positive, not negative. If you need to learn this attitude yourself, rent the movie *Pollyanna*. You'll both be playing the Glad Game in no time!

Keep burned-out light bulbs in their sockets until they are replaced, so baby won't be tempted to put a finger in the electrical socket. Keep lamps out of baby's reach to prevent accidental burns.

Become aware of these hazards now, before your baby is active enough to discover them himself.

L et your child be challenged. That's how he learns.

D on't underestimate your child, even if he is a baby. For example, if your baby has accompanied you in the car on the same roads every day for a few months, believe me—he remembers the way and could probably teach you.

Accept early that most babies won't always take their parents' word for everything. Some babies just want to learn things their way and we need to learn that not all lessons can be taught.

My first son, Michael Dean, never questioned anything. He played happily with safe toys and avoided any area that was threatening. If I said, "No!" even at five months, he'd become overwhelmed with guilt and drop whatever he was doing and immediately crawl across the floor back into my arms.

Then Brandon came along. Brandon was the first one to notice, at seven months old, that the cable cords behind the TV could be reached easiest by climbing straight through the bottom of the VCR shelf. And when I said, "No!" he would head in the other direction at about 90 miles an hour with a grin on his face that I can't describe without laughing.

Often, I would try to stop him from doing things, but then he would scream for his independence. If I did let him do it and he got hurt, he never seemed to cry as much as he did when I didn't let him try it. So I decided that it was OK to lose a few battles in order to win the war, as long as these battles were reasonably safe ones to lose.

Three years have gone by now and Brandon and I still have the same thing going on between us. Last January, on a 35-degree day in New Jersey, we drove to his childcare facility about four miles away and I forgot to secure the automatic window lock for the back seats. Within a few seconds of getting in the car, it was freezing. I looked in the rearview mirror at Brandon (with his perfectly adorable grin) and saw that he had opened his window from his car seat.

I said, "Brandon! It's freezing outside!" and without hesitation, I held down the driver's-side control button to raise the window. The next thing I knew, the window was down again because he had beat me to the button. My first reaction was to roll my eyes and think, "Here we go again. I can't stand it anymore!" but instead of doing anything, I just let him put the window down again, acting like I didn't know it was down. After about ten seconds, he closed the window again in a panic and said, "Mom, it is freezing outside!" And I said, "Yes, it is, and you are so smart, Brandon!"

Keep in mind the old adage: "It doesn't matter if you win or lose, it's how you play the game."

As a rule, babies learn from mistakes faster than their parents do.

As your baby grows, the best way to teach her to blow her nose is to cover her mouth for short intervals.

Teach your child to follow directions early. Being able to follow directions is an important skill for such things as cleaning up—and school!

When you clean up a room, remember to roam the floor at baby's level. Pick up any small objects baby might be inclined to swallow. Look for rough or splintered places along the molding—sand and repaint those spots.

Help your child learn to rely on himself.

Put down the baby! If you hold your baby too much, he'll never learn how to crawl or be alone.

Observe your child for signs of individuality. For example, one of my boys liked to be completely undressed and was miserable unless his feet were free. The other one had to be completely bundled up at all times.

Set an example

Have you ever noticed that babies who live with either cats or dogs learn to crawl at an earlier age? I think this is even more proof that babies watch and imitate everyone around them.

Consider your baby a video camcorder with a high-tech recording system. Everything you say is being registered. Your words, thoughts and expressions will be replayed for you at a later date.

If you notice you are missing a button or you've dropped something equally small, make a point to check baby's mouth and hands right away.

Your child watches you every day. He wants to be just like you and do what you do. While he is watching you brush your teeth, dab his tongue every now and then with your family brand of toothpaste. He'll be familiar with the flavor and ready to go by the time his teeth come in.

Remember, babies only grab at everything you have because they are imitating you.

Don't be surprised if you recognize your own faults in your baby. Sometimes it's like looking in the mirror—which can be pretty scary, huh?

Bugs amaze children. Never kill one in front of a child. Instead, gently move it outside in a paper towel or cup so it can "go home to its family."

Try not to argue with anyone, especially your spouse, in front of your child. You will see how much it upsets her, even at this early age. Teach your child to love and respect others by example.

If your child is home all day, take the time to put her in a position to see productive people doing productive things—starting with you! You are your baby's example, so be the best example you can be.

Make a commitment
to be a good parent.
You can never love
too much.

Start taking your child to your house of worship early. At an early age, he will learn about respect and how to be quiet.

Babies need to develop independence. It is our job as parents to show them how. For example, show your baby how to hold his bottle so he can drink from it (although never leave him alone with it). Babies can pick up a trick like shaking a rattle in two seconds at around four months; believe me, at around seven months, they can hold up their own bottle and probably want to.

Encourage and challenge

Applaud every time your baby stops what she is doing, looks at you and smiles. At that moment, she feels as though she has accomplished something—maybe she pulled herself up to stand and then let go and dropped back to the floor.

She is getting ready to take her first steps, and she needs your support! It's a little scary for her—how would you feel about trying a back-handspring right now for the first time?

To encourage your baby to try moving, put her favorite toys slightly out of reach.

Roadblock

I read my baby's horoscope recently and it said, "Enjoy spending quality time at home. You have been on the go for so long now that you need to learn how to relax. Good news! A roadblock in your way has graciously been removed." It was funny, because the day before, I had taken down the child's gate between the family room and the kitchen.

Each child has his own spirit. Enjoy your child's and do everything you can to protect and encourage it.

And yes, encourage assertiveness, but don't allow your child to dictate directions to others. After all, he's no expert—he has a lot to learn about life yet!

Try not to be overprotective. Most babies are naturally cautious, but keep an eye on them at all times, especially around a swimming pool. If you have a pool, a latched gate and a motion sensor are excellent ideas. A fence may be required by law.

If your baby slips and falls on her bottom in the bathtub, help her immediately, but calmly. Make her feel as though she helped herself. You will help your child build self-confidence and a sense of security. You will teach her to handle these startling situations without panicking.

Give your child the floor and let her show off at least once every day.

People were always telling me it would be "all over" once my child started crawling or walking. But life actually became easier at that point, because my son could get exactly what he wanted for himself. (More proof things tend to work out for the best!)

Some children never crawl. They go from sitting to standing to *running!*

Let your child learn cause and effect. Let him explore under your watchful eye and play with lots of toys.

Activities

Outdoors

Explore the outdoors with your child. The first time your child sees a bird, butterfly, puddle, a dog or a cat may be the first time you've really seen one, too.

Lighten up! Do something silly, like a cartwheel, in front of your child. It will crack her up! (Just make sure it doesn't crack you up, too!)

Don't forget to notice the wind! Watching the shaking branches of a tree is fun, and who knows, maybe the tree is trying to wave hello to us. Noticing the wind is the perfect way to encourage your child to use her imagination.

Make sure your baby sees the ocean and touches the sand whenever possible.

If you live far from an ocean, let your child touch the bark of a 100-year-old tree and roll in the grass every sunny day.

If you live in the city, no problem! My boys would trade anything to live in a place with so many wheels and trains. My niece would also pay a pretty price to live in an area where she could admire bridal gowns on display and other window-shopping delights.

The object is to make wherever you live fun (reading books about your area helps)!

Kids grow faster during the summer!

Let your child get dirty! Make sure he has plenty of play clothes, and I mean *play* clothes —the kind that can get dirty, torn and tossed, if need be.

Stop at the pet store! Your baby has been playing with stuffed animals for months—he would probably love to meet a real one.

The Fourth of July will be lots of fun starting at age three or so, but for now expect the loud firecrackers to bother your baby and make him scream.

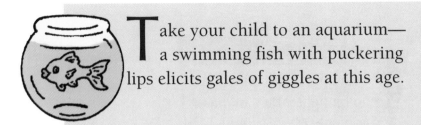

Take your child to an aquarium—a swimming fish with puckering lips elicits gales of giggles at this age.

It may take your baby several years to learn to swim, so start early. Six months is a good time to start, but not before.

Believe it or not, you have to grow a child. They need sunlight, fresh air and lots of water.

If it is warm outside, let your baby play in a baby pool in the morning (or give your baby a bath in the morning instead of the evening). It makes her hungry, wears her out —and it's fun!

Always get duplicates of photographs. You can make a separate photo album as your child grows and give it to him later in life, as a wedding gift perhaps.

G o look for a frog or a lizard with your baby! You'll be glad you did when you see him belly laugh at the way those little critters jump or run.

I f you drive by a park, stop and play! Fresh air revitalizes you and the baby.

Indoors

Every morning and afternoon, at a window facing the street, let your child watch the other youngsters in the neighborhood get on and off the school bus or walk to and from school.

Every now and then my grandmother used to tell me, "I made you eggs, oatmeal with sugar, and toast with butter for breakfast." Then she would give me an oatmeal cookie!

Babies love hats! Dress up yourself or the baby—either way, it's good for a few laughs. Collect all the hats you can, from baseball caps to snow hats. (The best part is that later you can use them again by giving them to your husband.)

Babies usually love the sound of running water, so bring your baby into the bathroom in a carrying seat while you take a shower. He will probably fall asleep. Later, all that running water helps with potty training.

Turn on the water and you are on your way to training!

 Reading and storytelling

S ome children want to hold books and look at the pictures just because they see their parents reading. This is the most wonderful kind of patterning!

C hoose a specific time every day to sit down together and read a book instead of watching TV.

R ead to your child *every day* at a certain time. You might choose to read a favorite comic strip when you sit down with the newspaper in the evening. Very soon this ritual will become your special time together with your child.

Use the weekly grocery-store or toy-store circular as a learning tool! Your child will love picking out the items he uses and sees so often at home with you. It's like getting a new book every week in the mail.

While you are naming pictures and reading to your child, don't forget to spell out some of the simple words.

Youngsters love to hear stories. It doesn't matter what the story is about. If you don't know a story, no problem—make one up! (That's what a story is.)

Music

Babies love sing-a-long videotapes and Richard Scarry's Busy Town™! series. Try them!

Teach your child to sing by singing to him!

When you sing "Twinkle, twinkle, Little Star" to your child, use your fingers to twinkle.

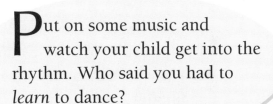

Put on some music and watch your child get into the rhythm. Who said you had to *learn* to dance?

In the kitchen

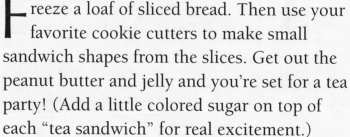

Freeze a loaf of sliced bread. Then use your favorite cookie cutters to make small sandwich shapes from the slices. Get out the peanut butter and jelly and you're set for a tea party! (Add a little colored sugar on top of each "tea sandwich" for real excitement.)

For "tea," serve lemonade (actually diluted lemon water): One lemon wedge squeezed into 8 to 10 ounces of water.

Forget exercise. To avoid a heart attack, keep all peanuts, popcorn, caramels and hard candy out of the house. They are choking hazards and babies will find them.

Don't allow these foods, or hot dogs, until your baby is well over three years old.

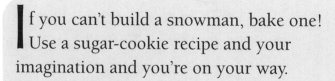

If you can't build a snowman, bake one! Use a sugar-cookie recipe and your imagination and you're on your way.

Toys

In about the third month, baby is getting ready for an activity. Best type of toy: One that hangs just high enough above her that she can learn how to kick and swat at things.

Don't forget, you are the best toy!

Get a mobile if you don't have one! Babies love to watch them and they're great for developing hand-foot coordination. The best mobile I've seen features frames made out of little cookie-cutter shapes. The frames can hold a picture of each member of your family.

Be sure to remove the mobile the minute your baby learns to stand up, because mobiles are dangerous when a baby can reach them from the crib.

Babies love rattles. Rattles help them build dexterity with their hands. Make sure you give your baby a variety to experiment with.

Musical toys such as xylophones and cymbals are usually a favorite with babies.

If you truly want to keep your baby occupied in a playpen, forget toys! Instead, give him the things you use all day—pots, pans, spoons, strainers and toothbrushes are all well-loved by little ones.

When your baby starts to get bored quickly, usually at seven or eight months, keep an activity center in the crib because the baby will wake up and play with it instead of cry. He will challenge himself to move and start to use the activities. In fact, I put one in the crib right from the start. If he wakes up with nothing to do, he will probably scream to get out of the crib. Wouldn't you?

Appropriate toys

Give your child the right toy at the right age. Toys and games usually have age-specific labels. Following the label is a good idea for a couple of reasons:

1

You can be sure the toy doesn't have small pieces that might choke a small child—a major concern.

2

You'll be sure the child is old enough to use the toy for its intended purpose. A child who receives a toy that is too "old" for her won't be able to play the game the way it is meant to be played. She will remember it as a frustrating experience and probably will never like it, even when she is older.

Children love anything tiny, and they especially like to put those tiny things in their mouths. To prevent choking, make sure that anything near your baby is bigger than her fist.

Baby's Favorite "Toy"

Babies are born to be investigators. They want to know everything about everything, especially toys, switches on television sets and other objects they see us using around the house. The length of time they spend on an object depends simply on how long it takes them to figure it out. Once they master the challenge, they move on to something else to conquer. Sound familiar?

Sometimes the most useless-looking objects can occupy your baby for hours, whereas a toy you spent tons of money on is of no interest to him. When my baby Brandon was about seven months old, he became completely enthralled with the little plastic lid of a sippy cup. It was bright pink and it fit perfectly into other things, so even though it didn't really do anything, he couldn't figure out what it was supposed to do, and that's what kept him occupied for months. Every time he had an opportunity to include it and try to get it to do something, he would race by all the other toys in the room to get it.

I remember the exact moment he realized it was just the lid to his cup. I could tell by the look on his face. After that, he spent the next few days trying intensely to figure out how to get it to snap on to the cup. Once he heard it click, he never played with it again.

If you instill a love of reading, puzzles, crayons and painting (with water) now, you will be able to keep your child occupied for hours between the ages of one and five.

Little Tykes® toys sell out at garage sales by 8:00 A.M. Shop early!

$ Here's a great toy for under ten dollars: a plastic sprinkler! This toy is terrific because it's fun at any age—your child can play with it too!

If your child is attached to a special toy or stuffed animal, try to get your hands on an exact duplicate, and never let the second one out of the house.

If you forget the original at a friend's house, lose it or it wears out, you'll have "old reliable" to pull out and save the day . . . or night, if the special "toy" happens to be a blanket.

Do you have a child-size slide in your yard? Clean it off and bring it into your baby's room for the winter months. It is also a great idea to bring a slide into the house during nighttime gatherings to give the kids something special to do.

Infants know who they are when they look into the mirror.

To maintain your child's interest in his toys, put away a few each time your child receives a new one. Bring them out again in six months.

If you want to get rid of some toys because you have too many, donate new or slightly used toys to local charities, schools, hospitals, places of worship and daycare centers.

Homemade toy ideas

These toys are for parents to use with baby, not for baby to play with on his own.

- A portable mobile made from a hanger, tissue or bright towel, and yarn

- A brightly colored kitchen towel

- Dishwashing liquid makes great bubbles

- Good old paper airplanes

- Flashlights

- Anything round that can roll, such as an orange or a small can of peas. (Playing with things they see you buy at the grocery store is especially fun for babies because they are usually locked into their chair and can't reach anything from the shopping cart. They will remember what you buy and later be delighted if you bring them out as "toys.")

- Pots, pans and wooden spoons, especially for playing in the kitchen while you cook (they love to imitate their parents and they *love* the noise)

- Plastic containers with lids (much quieter than pots and pans—perfect for playpen fun)

- Nonbreakable mirror (with supervision!)

- Make a cassette tape with baby and play it back during playtime, while she rests or when you leave her with a baby-sitter, so she can hear familiar family sounds. (Videotapes work great too!)

- Cardboard box as a tunnel for baby to crawl through

Communication

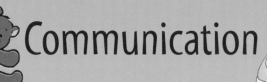

As usual, communication is the key to success. There's a philosophy in business that says, "If I don't hear anything from you, everything's fine or you're up to something." I'm not sure about business, but it's definitely true with babies.

There's also the old saying "The squeaky wheel gets the oil," and that's what I think of sometimes when my baby is crying. It is, after all, the only way my baby can let me know that he needs something.

To communicate with your baby, you have to watch and learn from his tones, body language and levels of stress. And believe me, he will learn from yours. I've noticed that when I'm trying to get my baby to stop crying by rocking him on my shoulder, if my neck is tightened up, he gets more angry. I believe that he can tell I'm tense and he's counting on me to help him. If this happens, I take deep breaths to get myself to relax—basically, so I won't end up crying, too.

Your baby is always communicating with you. Notice the little things. Whenever I see my baby dancing his feet, I know he's happy, and I don't change a single thing.

Body Language

To communicate love

Babies don't know how to hide their emotions . . . and most parents don't know how to *show* their emotions. Spend time with your baby and say "I love you" as many times a day as you can.

The more your baby feels loved, the happier she usually is. Hugs are one of the best things in life! Hug your new baby and tell her you love her as often as you can, especially if she is crying. Remember, your baby is trying to reach out to you and communicate without knowing how to talk.

In fact, make it a habit to hug each member of your family every day. Tell them you love them and how important they are to you . . . especially through their teenage years.

Fun with Body Language

Have fun and establish private jokes with your child. For instance, your baby may smile every time you wink your eye, raise your eyebrow or make biting noises with your teeth. You can use these special signals to entertain your child when she is cranky and you are stuck somewhere without a toy (a line at the grocery store or in the car waiting to pick up Dad).

Babies like to be bounced gently, not shaken or patted too hard. Shaking or patting a baby too hard can severely injure him—or worse.

To communicate a bad mood

Babies get cranky from overstimulation. So do adults!

Baby powder is one of the best ways to cool down an irritable child. If you live in a warm climate, carry a bottle with you so you will always be ready if your baby becomes uncomfortable.

Another plus: It works just as well on you!

If you are having a bad day, expect baby to be having one, too.

A great way to test your baby for overstimulation is to keep a pinwheel in your diaper bag. This is a tiny paper toy on a straw that, when blown, whirls around like a fan. You can get them at any five-and-dime. If your baby is impatient, pull out the pinwheel. If he loves it, he's bored. If he hates it, he's tired and overstimulated, which means you should put him down for a nap. Too much is going on!

If your baby is in a really bad mood, pretend he is a stressed-out grown-up caught in a rush-hour traffic jam. People can be really nasty in that kind of situation until you smile at them. But usually, once you do, they smile back—and even wave!

Regular periods of crankiness are baby's way of burning off stress, so be grateful for them! They usually only last until baby is as used to the real world as he was to the womb.

☆ Sanity Tip

Put an auto reply on your email that tells people you are on maternity leave. Also change all outgoing voicemail and answering-machine messages to say that you only collect incoming messages on your home telephone line. Let your answering machine or voicemail catch incoming calls while your baby is awake. And then, "accidentally" forget to change your voice mail for about a year!

While your baby is sleeping, you will have time to return calls and emails rather than spending the entire nap collecting messages from all of your different telephone lines and computers.

S ometimes parents think their baby is just "always cranky." Often the baby is simply frustrated because she can't talk and get her point across. In these cases, the baby gets nicer as she gets older and learns to speak.

Then again, some babies end up proving that their parents were absolutely right: You just have to wait and see!

Mixed Messages

At church last week, I laughed so hard because this new mother had a seven-month-old that she kept rotating around from the car seat, to her lap, to her shoulder, to the car seat, to her husband and so on. She never realized that every time the baby leaned down, the only thing he wanted was the *Spot* book that was clearly visible to him in her diaper bag, which sat on the floor. She thought he just wanted to get down, so she continued to move him from place to place throughout the service. I couldn't just call out to her, of course, although I wanted to tell her, "Hey, he doesn't want to get down. He's just trying to reach that book!"

To communicate thoughts

If your baby just looks at you without expression, even when you are trying to get him to smile, he is probably concentrating. He may be studying something new about your face. Or he may be having a bowel movement. He is *not* thinking you are an idiot.

Once your baby starts dropping toys outside the playpen and hurling stuffed animals over the side of the crib, I suspect he is thinking, "You first—I'm right behind you!"

If you hear a loud thump on the monitor, check it out fast. Your baby may have decided the risk was worth the reward and climbed out of his crib.

Don't worry too much. Humans have an instinctive fear of falling. Most babies won't have anywhere near the courage to climb out until they are about 36 inches tall or two years old. And whatever you do, don't rush your baby out of the crib. You'll be giving yourself another part-time job when you work three already!

If your baby leans toward you with an open mouth, she is probably hungry . . . but she may be trying to give you a kiss!

Word to the wise: If it's an important day and the baby *must* look great, she will either scratch her face or get a bad haircut.

If your baby rubs her eyes *or* moves her head back and forth, she's probably trying to say, "No, not this activity. Let's try something else and I'll be fine. If I'm not, give me a nap please."

Hit the Bed

Everything you do, your baby
watches and tries to imitate.
Here's a classic example:

First of all, I confess that I am a bed fanatic. I have
to make my bed every morning and it doesn't matter if I
know I am going to take a nap later. My habit annoys
everyone in our house—including me!

Anyway, during this one period of my life, Brandon
was driving me crazy. Every time I would just finish
making the bed, he would either crawl up to it, pull up
on it and then hit it or, after he learned to walk, he'd run
up to it and hit it. After praying for sanity and patience, it
occurred to me one day that he wasn't *hitting* the bed at
all. He was trying to straighten it, in the exact same spot
that I always do.

So keep in mind that you may not
always recognize their impersonation of
you right away.

Crying

Why?

People have said for years that babies beg for boundaries and that this applies to everything from eating to playing to sleeping. It wasn't until I had my second child that I realized they were speaking literally: Babies do actually beg. They scream and cry. Notice if your baby cries in the same tone whenever he is hungry, tired or bored.

From the very beginning, babies learn to cry in different tones when they want different things. Watch for these distinguishing cries and you will learn what they need. (Most important, you will also be able to tell the difference between their normal needs and when they are in pain.)

Babies cry when they are hungry, wet, bored, sick, tired or just to relieve stress . . . so do postpartum moms!

B abies cry just as hard when they are tired and want to go to bed as they do when they are hungry and want to eat.

Keep hot beverages out of baby's arm's-length reach. You don't realize how quick babies are until they have spilled something hot and burned themselves.

N ot sure why baby's crying? Well, keep in mind that babies *don't* like

- Overstimulation
- Changes in their routines
- Loud and abrupt noises
- Tense parents

I f your baby is a "whiner," you are probably responsible, unfortunately. To break her of this habit, have her spend more time with others. She may be whiny because she is too dependent on you.

Babies and Noise

Recently my sister had a birthday party for my seven-year-old niece. My other niece, who is just eight months old, was as happy as could be sitting in the highchair at the table with all the other little girls at the party. The six boys, my two included, sat at another table about five feet away.

The boys table was LOUD and filled with battling action figures. The girls table was filled with quiet excitement while the cake was being prepared.

When my sister was ready to get the party rolling, she said, "OK, are you guys ready to sing, 'Happy Birthday'?" And when the girls yelled, "Yes!" all at the same time, the baby freaked out and screamed for about an hour and a half straight.

The moral of this story, of course, is that while babies can adjust to a constant stream of noise, they hate *abrupt* loud noises.

T ry not to make abrupt moves around your infant. Startled babies create a crying frenzy.

Babies remind me of rainbows because they usually show up shining brilliantly after a storm.

A fter a baby has been crying uncontrollably for a little while, she may have forgotten *why* she is crying. Try rocking, dancing or singing. And stay calm!

When to let baby cry

It's OK to let your baby cry for a little while sometimes. Crying is actually good for babies. Some say it helps develop their lungs.

All babies are good; some just cry more than others.

Try not to run to the rescue every time your baby becomes frustrated or cries. Let him first try to work out his problems for himself. Your restraint, difficult though it may be, is especially important when you are helping your baby learn to sleep through the night.

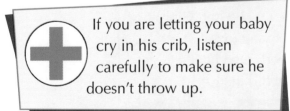

If you are letting your baby cry in his crib, listen carefully to make sure he doesn't throw up.

Speech

Encouraging speech

As your child grows, look for opportunities to help him learn. For example, if you ask your son to hand you the silverware and he just stares at you, ask for forks and spoons instead. Children's vocabularies are only as broad as you make them.

Instead of talking to yourself, tell your child everything you are thinking. Give him descriptive words so he can increase his vocabulary.

Be quiet when your baby is trying to talk. He needs the chance to get a word in.

U se the "magic words" around your baby and to your baby at all times. In case you have forgotten, the magic words include *please, excuse me, thank you* and *you're welcome.*

I f you use bad language around your baby, don't be surprised by her first words.

B abies who are introduced to foreign languages can actually learn languages much easier later. Try putting a foreign-language radio station on low volume during a quiet time, perhaps while baby is in the crib. Just don't be surprised if her first words are "Buenos Días, Mama!"

If your child is quiet, she is probably getting into something.

As your child learns to talk, you will become a good translator. Notice that phrases such as, "Please, Mom, please!" mean he knows he shouldn't have whatever it is he is asking for.

Just because you don't understand what your baby is saying doesn't mean your baby doesn't understand what *you* are saying.

For the next couple of years, as your child is learning to talk, he will only tell the truth. Children do not learn to fib until much later. If you hear a child make observations such as "you're fat" . . . well, maybe your child is gifted.

Being around a child has many advantages. One is that you will receive a totally objective opinion in every situation.

When I was about twenty-four years old, I worked as an administrative assistant for my dad part time. One day, when I joined him on a sales call, the executive we were meeting with decided to ask me a few questions. I didn't really know what I was talking about, but I acted like I knew everything anyway.

After the meeting, my dad said to me, "Jeanne, there's nothing wrong with saying, 'I don't know,' when you don't know the answer to something. Believe me, it will make your life a lot easier."

It's important to realize that most people don't feel comfortable *offering* advice on parenting to new parents because it's such a personal experience. Parenting isn't taught in school. Everyone has different values and beliefs. There are some rights and wrongs but few written rules.

Ask for help when you need it, and ask for suggestions when you want to consider them. But above all, don't forget: "There's nothing wrong with saying, 'I don't know,' when you don't know the answer to something. Believe me, it will make your life a lot easier!"

To illustrate why "I don't know" is sometimes the best answer, here are some questions I'm always asked: "Did you ever let your babies cry?" and "How long do you let a baby cry?" The only answer I can give is "Yes, I did let my babies cry and *I don't know* how long YOU should let YOUR baby cry because that's your decision."

I knew when my children needed to rest and I let my children cry long enough to teach them that just because they cried, didn't mean that I would change my mind, but short enough so they didn't get sick or think I didn't adore them. And all I can say is that they always woke up loving me just as much as they did *before* I started letting them cry.

Baby Meets World

There is nothing better in life than family and friends, and it is our job as parents to help our children grow up having them. Our friends make us smile, teach us to share, give us love and, sometimes, even wear us out. To that end, they are even more important for babies than I had thought!

As your baby grows, do what you can to introduce her to all types of people, and teach her love and forgiveness. Even babies as young as newborns can tell when their parents do not care for someone, so try not to talk about anyone negatively around them and try to be a good example from the first day home from the hospital. Remember the old rule: "If you can't say anything nice, don't say anything at all," because your baby will pick it up, repeat it and use it against you later.

Introduce your baby to others early because your baby will enjoy it immensely and every relationship will teach her new things about trust and love. This is even true with her baby-sitters and childcare providers. Remember, babies love people, even if they don't like being *left* with people, at first.

Going Out

Should you bring baby?

Be advised: If you attend a social event with a child under two years old, you will be spending your time in a quiet room, parking lot or park—not at the party.

If you plan a night out with your husband, don't use it as an opportunity to call a family grievance meeting. Save that for the next morning and enjoy yourself!

If anyone invites you to a gathering and uses the expression, "Bringing your baby is up to you," immediately respond with, "Oh, we will definitely get a baby-sitter."

If you buy your child a ticket to any event, be sure the performance lasts no longer than three minutes.

If no one else is bringing children, don't bring yours.

What should you bring for baby?

When you go to another person's home, bring along something your baby is familiar with—an activity gym, for example. This way, if she gets cranky, you can give her a familiar, soothing object until she calms down.

Invest your next couple of extra dollars in the greatest invention ever made for a mother—a remote-controlled car-starting device. With this gadget, you can start your car and warm it up on cold mornings from inside the house while you're still packing up the baby.

Keep a stroller, walking device and portable playpen in the car. (They are a pain to carry around, but believe me, it's worth it.)

Use safety gates, but not the accordian-fold type or the kind used to contain pets.

Bring along the gate when you visit others' homes. If they don't have one and your baby can crawl, your visit will last only about five minutes.

If you are going somewhere quiet, such as a library or a place of worship, make sure to bring along a pacifier or something your child can suck on. As your child gets older, add a lollipop or chewy snack. Those really keep little mouths busy!

Sanity Tip

If someone gives you an outfit, put it on your baby the next time they visit. They will know you appreciated it and maybe they'll give you another one a couple sizes larger when they realize your baby will soon outgrow it.

Also, if anyone ever asks you what size your baby is wearing, add on at least two sizes. Then, if you can't visit them for a while, you're baby will still fit in the clothes they gave you when you do see them again.

Diaper bag essentials

- Hat
- Blanket
- Backup nipple, pacifier and bottle
- Portable fan
- Breast pump or powdered formula backup
- Baby powder
- A few diapers and wipes
- Sunscreen: SPF 15 or higher
- Backup set of clothing
- Pain reliever

Also, it's good to travel with

- Age-appropriate toys
- Portable crib

Teaching Baby Good Social Skills

Baby and other adults

If someone you trust wants to play with your baby, say, "Sure, take your time!"

Don't leave your child with a person too old, too young or too dumb.

If you don't want anyone to touch your baby, that's OK. If you can't seem to say so directly, just say the baby isn't feeling well and you don't want to risk spreading a virus.

If your child wants to get down and go when you are trying to hold him on your lap, save yourself a lot of trouble by letting him down to play. Don't be too apologetic. Other parents usually understand these things.

Babies are actually around nine months old the day they are born!

Some babies love older folks, so visit older relatives or stop by a nursing home—it will brighten *everyone's* day. Your visit also provides a good opportunity to teach your children to treat older adults with respect.

Of course, some babies are completely terrified of the elderly. My second son, Brandon, was that way, so when he got nervous, I'd say, "Look at Grandpa! Isn't he lucky that he gets to ride in a big-boy stroller?"

D on't overdress your baby just to visit a friend or go to the grocery store. How would *you* like it if you had to wear a business suit on your day off? Keep your baby comfortable and your life will be the same.

If you have a hectic morning schedule, dress your baby the night before to save a little time in the morning.

S tart now to teach your child to leave other people's knickknacks alone when visiting their house. Watch him carefully and remind him as needed until this idea is ingrained in his head: *You can't play with everything everywhere you go!*

Baby and other children

If you want a good child, keep good children in her company . . . and remember the reverse.

Parents are subjective when it comes to their child, no matter how hard they try not to be. And this is wonderful. Always stick up for your child unless you *know* she is in the wrong.

Teach your child how to visit friends and spend the night at another person's house early in life. This will prevent a lot of midnight pickups and interrupted date nights for you later on.

$ Get together with your friends and swap your children's toys now and then. To a child, no toy is better than someone else's. To a parent, no toy is cheaper than borrowing someone else's.

Always buy the same food for every child in the car, and buy the same toy for every child in the room from now on.

You can take the person out of the situation, but you can't take the situation out of the person—except with babies! If your baby's unhappy with a person or situation, just leave. He won't dwell on it. He'll already be thinking about what to do next!

Children this age bite everything—but they shouldn't bite everyone. If your baby bites others, call your doctor right away and take steps to stop this behavior. Biting jeopardizes the welfare of both children and is never acceptable.

When Company Comes

If company is over and you meet your husband in the baby's room for a private conversation, don't forget . . . the monitor is always on!

The mother's rule of thumb for entertaining guests with children is to "clean up afterward, not before."

☆ Sanity Tip

If your baby's outfit is just a little too big but you want him to wear it anyway, wash it first and throw it into the dryer to shrink it.

Babies wiggle! And for that reason, a baby will fall off any counter she is put on. Always place babies safely on the floor, no matter what kind of carrying device or seat they are secured in.

If you throw a party or some other event, remember the baby is not used to so much company. She may become overstimulated from all the different people who want to hold her. At some point, go into a quiet room, remove her diaper, clothes and socks and give her some quiet space for twenty minutes. This works great and will revitalize her for another round!

If you're having guests over and you want to keep everything neat, give your baby a bath until the guests arrive. This way, she is contained in one area and clean, along with the house, when your friends arrive.

Family

Some family members, especially grandparents, genuinely want to become close to your baby. Don't deprive your child or your relatives of this joy. Besides all its other benefits, the relationship will help your child learn how to love others.

If you have a small family but good friends, call them "aunt, uncle and cousin" for your child's sake.

✰ Sanity Tip

The best way for everyone in the family to keep sane is simply to move outside. Fresh air is the key to *everyone's* sanity.

If you are concerned about leaving your fussy baby with your parents overnight, consider this: Babies usually behave better with others than they do with their own parents. So go ahead, try it!

Traveling with Baby

Give your baby a pacifier or bottle just before takeoff on an airplane. This will get him to swallow and relieve the pressure in his ears.

Organize clothing in Ziploc® bags ahead of time.

If you are planning an airplane trip, keep your child awake in the car on the way to the airport. For the sake of everyone else on the plane, don't let him fall asleep until you get on board.

☆ Sanity Tip

Mom, are you stressed out? Consider this: Standard airline procedure tells parents to place an emergency oxygen mask over our own mouths first, if extra oxygen is needed in the cabin. Only after that are we to put a mask over our child's mouth. Only after *our* needs are met are we *physically able* to take care of our child's needs.

It's not too different at home. For the family to be happy, Mom needs to take care of herself as well as her family. . . . Get some fresh air now and then!

The best way to warm a bottle when traveling is to ask a waiter for a large cup of hot water and then drop the bottle into the cup for about one minute to heat it. You can also bring your own thermos of boiling water.

Baby powder helps remove sand after you go to the beach, and hair after baby's first haircut.

Use sunscreen (both you and baby) and try to stay out of the sun between 12:00 and 3:00 P.M.

Only bring enough diapers to get you where you want to go and then buy a package of them when you get there. This will save space.

If you're visiting a friend who doesn't have a quiet baby room, try going into the bathroom, turn off the lights and turn on the vented ceiling fan while nursing or snuggling your baby to sleep.

Newborn babies like brightly colored objects, so a bright washcloth (that fits nicely in your diaper bag) will keep your baby occupied if you throw it up where she can look at it.

It's always good to keep a pain-relieving medication such as Motrin® or Tylenol® in your diaper bag while traveling—if you need it, you'll have it.

Baby-Sitters

Choosing a caregiver

Make sure you've seen your baby smile at her caregiver at least once.

If your baby-sitter hangs around to visit with the family after she's been paid, consider adopting her!

Keep in mind that times change. For example, nowadays your baby-sitter will want to read *your* resumé before she accepts the job, just as much as you wish to read hers before you offer her the position.

If you need a baby-sitter for an extended period, try using two baby-sitters who split the work. This idea works especially well if you have a helpful family. Use your sitter for the first half and a family member for the second. The baby is kept busy, it's cheaper and no one becomes exhausted!

Leaving your child with a caregiver

Babies love to watch their family members do *anything*. If you leave your child with a sitter, leave videotapes of your family, too. If the baby gets cranky, your sitter can play the tape, and voilá—instant comfort and familiarity! Just remember . . . the baby will probably be fine and the *sitter* will watch the tape.

Give your home an early safety check. See it from your baby's viewpoint! For instance, check out your fireplace. Keep those heavy fire pokers and other dangerous accessories out of baby's reach. Remove matches or other fire starters. If you have a gas fireplace, remove the gas key.

You'll be glad you did later.

If you trust your baby-sitter, don't show up early more than once or twice, here and there.

If you have a good sitter and you arrive on time instead of early, you may not have to straighten up the house!

If you drop off your child at a daycare center and she throws a fit, don't spend all day feeling guilty. If it's a good daycare center (one you've checked out carefully), your baby will probably stop crying as soon as you're gone. Don't prolong the agony by hanging around. Out of sight, out of mind!

Show (and tell) your baby every day how much you love her.

If you leave your child for more than twenty-four hours with a baby-sitter, don't be surprised if she treats the baby-sitter like her mother and you like her baby-sitter for twenty-four hours after you return. It's normal; babies adjust to their environment. Instead of feeling unhappy, be glad your baby is so adaptable!

Leave the baby-sitter exact instructions for reaching you in an emergency. Make copies of the form on the next page.

Don't call the baby-sitter every hour after you go out. If you don't think your sitter is capable enough to use the instructions, don't leave your child with that sitter.

Emergency Instructions for Baby-Sitters

Date:

Where we'll be between the hours of _____ and _____:
   Name:
   Address:

   Telephone:

Where we'll be between the hours of _____ and _____:
   Name:
   Address:

   Telephone:

We are wearing:

Emergency Phone Numbers
Police: Ambulance:
Doctor—name: _____ and number: _____
Hospital—name: _____ and number: _____

Our address:

Nearest major intersections:

Backup telephone numbers of neighbors and relatives:

_____
name   number

_____
name   number

_____
name   number

At the bottom of this form, write in or attach the following:
• Your baby's hospital admission cards
• A letter authorizing care in your absence
• Your baby's schedule
• A to-do list in case of emergency

Mom's Tales

Whatever you do, make a vow today, right here and now with me as your witness, that you won't believe everything you hear.

New moms are often kind of "paranoid" for a very short period of time—about a year. You will hear something that's happened to some other child, and you will think it 100 percent pertains to your baby. I did the same thing. That's why I know this. All it does is cause you days of unnecessary fear, guilt and anguish.

If you ever get to this point, you have four action steps to implement:

1. Consider it as a possibility.
2. Check it out with your doctor.
3. File it as a "Mom's Tale" in your mind, along with the other "old wives' tales."
4. Never use it to torment or terrorize another new mom.

The most important thing I can tell you is that you have to learn to trust your instincts, which is kind of like taking a test: Usually, your first answer is the right answer. That's what instinct is all about.

Your mind will help you decide when a Mom's Tale is true . . . for you.

Best wishes and lots of love,

Tale: Baths put babies to sleep early when they're infants, and then keep them up and stimulate them as toddlers.

Not true! Baths are as much a routine as eating, sleeping and reading. Their purpose doesn't change.

Tale: Your firstborn is usually sensitive and caring, but your secondborn is usually strong willed. This is supposed to be because they have someone a little bit ahead of them to show them the ropes so they are more confident.

I believe this totally.

Tale: You can't get pregnant while you breastfeed.

Tell that to my cousin, my sister, my aunt, . . .

Tale: A fat baby is a healthy baby.

The sad truth is that fat babies often turn out to be overweight as adults . . . and that's very scary for me, because I was kind of a fat baby! However, babies do *not* need to diet. Discuss your baby's weight with your pediatrician if you are concerned.

Tale: The only time there is a black sheep in a family is when the parent calls a child a black sheep.

I believe this, too.

Tale: Flashbulbs are dangerous to baby and should not be used.

Taking flash pictures is perfectly safe.

Tale: Air conditioning is harmful for a baby.

How ridiculous! I can't even think of one hospital without an air-conditioning system.

Tale: Chicken soup cures the flu and common colds.

Maybe it doesn't actually *cure* anything, but there's some truth to this tale. The steam from the soup soothes congestion like a vaporizer.

Tale: Teething causes a high fever.

This is not always true. Some children don't get any fever at all. I never even noticed when half of my children's teeth came in because there were no symptoms at all. See your doctor about any temperature above 101 degrees.

Tale: Something is wrong with your baby if he gets his teeth late.

Definitely not. There's no connection between the time your baby's teeth come in and his development, physical, mental or otherwise.

Tale: Brushing babies' hair at night makes them sleep through the night faster.

I love it, so I believe it!

Tale: Baby will walk sooner if she wears shoes.

Actually, a barefoot baby will strengthen her muscles more and learn to walk sooner.

Tale: A baby between four and six months is insecure and unloved if strangers scare her.

Pure bologna. I'm twenty-eight, I know some people who love me and I'm still afraid of strangers! This fear is perfectly normal for babies, too.

    P.S. Remember: Don't believe everything you hear! I'm not really twenty-eight. I just wish I were.

Tale: When you scratch your baby's back, your baby learns to stand up tall in life and defend his positions.

I like this idea! I'm trying it!

Tale: If a baby stands too soon, she'll be bow-legged.

Of course not.

Remember, you can never be too safe. Often times, our grandparents remind us of how they didn't have all these safety concoctions and they got by just fine. Well, that's true—it's just that they didn't have all of the hazards we have like pools, VCRs, electrical sockets and, in some cases, even indoor toilets. When this comes up, I always remind people that my grandmother always says, "Better safe than sorry."

Tale: If your baby starts off a screamer, she will always scream, but it's because she knows what she wants.

Makes sense.

Tale: Babies with thick, dark hair at birth end up blonde at around two.

Seems entertaining, if nothing else, but I know a lot of people who would prove this otherwise.

Tale: Babies' eyes change color from blue to brown within the first year.

I've seen it take up to three years for eye color to change.

Baby's First Birthday!

As your baby grows, you are going to get all kinds of gifts from people for birthdays, holidays and special occasions—whether you want them or not.

A great way to keep sane is to have a "theme"—not only for the party, but for the gifts. Tell everyone close to you to give your baby one piece from a certain good quality toy. For instance, every year my family gives my baby a piece from the Thomas Tank Engine collection because he's basically obsessed. There is nothing more important to him than a new $5.00 wooden train piece.

I know it sounds a little controversial because people feel like they have to spend a fortune on birthday gifts. A few of my relatives were reluctant at first, but after they saw him run past several $20.00 toys with pure joy over receiving "Percy" from a friend of mine, they *all* came around.

Talk to your fellow parents and start this type of gift-giving. You will delight the children you love—your baby and your friends' children—and you'll also save a ton!

By the way, this only gets more true for children as they grow. They would prefer one good Barbie® outfit for their favorite doll or one $4.00 Hot Wheels® collector car than several toys they can't use or don't get into. Books related to their theme are also sure winners!

"Goodie bags" are only good for children three or older who just want the candy—or for their parents! Children under three just want the bag because someone else is holding it. They don't really think about the candy inside.

$ Save yourself a lot of money on your baby's upcoming one-year birthday party and just wrap a couple of empty boxes. Tearing off the paper will be your baby's favorite part of the day, anyway!

For Baby

It's a great idea to plan part of the baby's first birthday party around her nap because then you can visit with your guests! But don't forget, if all of your friends have babies, everyone may be sleeping through your party.

Let them eat cake!

Don't plan to give your child his first piece of birthday cake on his actual birthday. He could get sick and he probably won't like it. Instead, try giving it to him one week earlier and get him used to it. By the time his party rolls around, he will really enjoy a little birthday cake.

Don't spend a fortune on favors for your one-year-old's birthday party. The only favor your little guests need is the party, believe me.

I remember when our first baby, Michael Dean, turned one. We did everything, including hire a band for the event! My husband brought in a pony from a nearby farm for the other children, who were mostly under three, while I planted flowers in the garden, cleaned like a freak, bought enough food to feed China and expected everyone to be in a glorious mood.

Well, the babies were terrified of the pony, which stressed out all of the parents. No one noticed the flowers because it ended up raining. There were all these babies crawling around everywhere in the house—except our baby, who slept through most of the party. By 5:00 P.M., the other parents were so tired that no one stayed long enough to eat the food or hear the band. Doesn't that sound like a lot of fun? And it only cost $800!

Baby Basics

How to Clip Baby's Nails

I can't believe we can live on the earth for like 20 or 30 years and never really think deeply about clipping nails, yet along comes baby and it becomes a full-time job. Babies grow so fast that their nails need to be clipped two or three times a week!

First, you need to have a couple high quality nail clippers in different sizes: One size does *not* fit all. In fact, baby will grow through about two sizes in the first year alone. This is a big deal because if you cut your baby accidentally you will feel so bad that I can't describe it and your baby (and you) will start developing a fear of nail clipping.

On top of dealing with a child's fear, it could take you literally hours to get through all ten fingers and ten toes when your baby becomes a toddler. And then she will hurt herself with her own nails! Here's how to do it safely and how to get your baby to put her fingers up to you when you're ready to cut:

1

I can't stress this enough: Get a few pairs of good nail clippers in *various sizes*, beginning with infant size. If you use the correct size, you should only have to clip once because the curve will fit her fingers, and this will greatly reduce the risk of injury. Keep a file on hand at all times (in the diaper bag) to smooth off rough edges or to use instead of a clipper if you're not the gentle type.

2

Try to clip baby's nails when she is sleeping. If you are sleeping while she's sleeping and you forget, clip your baby's nails immediately after a bath because they will be softer and easier to cut.

3

Don't try to cut too low because you may take the skin by accident and this is what will cause pain and fear.

4

Let your baby watch you cut *your* nails first and smile all the while—even if you cut yourself.

5

Don't set a bad example and bite your nails—or your baby's.

How to Bathe Baby

Babies don't go into standard size bathtubs (unless you are holding them) until they can sit up (make sure you use a bath-ring seat at that point). It's very common for people to use a sink to bathe their baby, which is fine if it's clean. The problems start when the baby is quick enough to turn the faucet to hot or cold, or the parent underestimates the baby and the baby climbs (or falls) out. This happens unexpectedly any time after three months, so don't risk it. Use a baby bathtub or get into the bath with your baby to clean him.

 Never leave your baby alone for a second in the tub. Babies can drown in 2 inches of water.

Basic bathing steps:

1

For the first few days, you can just sponge off your baby with a clean washcloth and some mild soap while holding him on a sturdy surface.

2

To clean the umbilical cord, use cotton swabs and basic rubbing alcohol.

3

Always clean your baby's eyes first, working from the corner out with only warm water.

4

Don't be surprised if your baby urinates on you or himself while you're cleaning him off. Just start over if that happens.

5

After you clean his whole body with a soft cloth, apply a diaper and dress him warmly. It's nice to use baby powder after a bath, but using nothing is absolutely fine, too!

6

As baby grows and the cord falls off, you can hold him carefully under the sink and rinse him off if you are coordinated enough.

Despite what people have tried to tell me, I don't think newborns like being bathed. Once they are a few weeks old and can sit in their little bathtub (or in the tub with you) and feel completely

continued . . .

submerged in warm water, then they actually begin to like it. They probably don't like being held upside down naked, having one piece of their body at a time cleaned off like a turkey being prepared for Thanksgiving. They are used to a warm womb, after all. So if your baby cries, don't be surprised. Get through the cleaning quickly and get him dressed warmly. Once he can enjoy his bath, bathing gets easier.

Baths are a blessing. Give your baby a bath as often as you can.

Last Thought

The roots of a tree
are the most important part
They are the base and the place
where its character starts.

If the roots of the tree
are planted deep in the ground,
no matter the weather
the tree will be sound.

Let's plant the right seeds in our children now
so they will have deep and healthy roots.

Resources

See our website for resource updates and other great tips for parents! www.fisherbooks.com
Contact the author! babytips@worldnet.att.net

Breastfeeding

Breastfeeding.com
www.breastfeeding.com

International Lactation Consultant Association
4101 Lake Boone Trail, Ste. 201
Raleigh, NC 27607
919-787-5181

La Leche League International
1400 N. Meacham Rd.
Schaumburg, IL 60173
Tel: 800-LA-LECHE, 847-519-7730
Fax: 847-519-0035
www.lalecheleague.org

Ligue La Leche
CP874 St. Laurent
Quebec H4L 4W3
514-327-6714

Childcare

Au Pair in America
102 Greenwich Ave.
Greenwich, CT 06830
800-9AU-PAIR
www.aifs.com

Child Care Aware
800-424-2246

Families and Work Institute
330 Seventh Ave.
New York, NY 10001
212-465-2044

International Nanny Association
Station House, Ste. 438
900 Haddon Ave.
Collingswood, NJ 08108
Tel: 609-858-0808
Fax: 609-858-2519
www.nanny.org

National Association of Family Child Care
1331-A Pennsylvania Ave., Ste. 348
Washington, DC 20004
800-359-3817

National Child Care Information Center (NCCIC)
301 Maple Ave. W., Ste. 602
Vienna, VA 22180
Tel: 800-616-2242
Fax: 800-716-2242
ericps.ed.uiuc.edu/nccic/abtnccic.html

General Parenting

Baby Bag Online
www.babybag.com/

Baby Center
www.babycenter.com

Between Moms
www.cadvision.com/moms/

dads.com
www.dads.com/

Dadsite of the Month
www.concentric.net/~Bbickel/dadsite.html

Daily Parent
www.dailyparent.com/

The Family Education Network
familyeducation.com

Family Internet
www.familyinternet.com/

Family Planet
www.family.com

Family Resource Coalition
200 S. Michigan Ave.
16ᵀᴴ Floor
Chicago, IL 60604
312-341-0900

Family Resource Online
www.familyresource.org/

Family Service Canada
600-220 Laurier Ave.
West Ottawa, ON K1P 5Z9
613-230-9960

FamilyWeb
www.familyweb.com/

Fatherhood Project
c/o Families and Work Institute
330 7TH Ave., 14TH Floor
New York, NY 10001
212-465-2044
www.fatherhoodproject.org/

Kid Source
www.kidsource.com

Mommy Times
www.mommytimes.com/

MOMS Club
25371 Rye Canyon Rd.
Valencia, CA 91355
Moms supporting moms. Write for information packet. Please enclose $2 to cover costs.

Moms Online
www.momsonline.com

National Center for Fathering
fathers.com

National Clearinghouse on Families and Youth
(NCFY)
P.O. Box 13505
Silver Spring, MD 20911-3505
Tel: 301-608-8098
Fax: 301-608-8721
www.acf.dhhs.gov/programs/acyf/

National Fatherhood Initiative
www.register.com/father/

The National Parent Information Network
npin.org

Natural Child Project
www.naturalchild.com/

New Mothers Resource Group
c/o Anne Fownes
Box 1271
Liverpool, Nova Scotia B0T 1K0
902-354-2479

New Parents Network, Inc.
P.O. Box 64237
Tucson, AZ 85728-4234
Tel: 520-327-1451
Fax: 520-881-7104
Email: moreinfo@npn.org

Parent Education Ring
www.ksu.edu/wwparent/parentring.htm

Parent Helpline
800-942-4357

Parent News
parent.net/

Parent Soup
www.parentsoup.com

Parent Time
www.pathfinder.com/ParentTime/homepage/
    homepage.all.html

Parenthood Web
www.parenthoodweb.com

Parenting Helpline
800-531-5151

Parenting Links
www.ark.org/kidz/parents.html

Parenting Matters
lifematters.com/parentn.html

Parenting Q & A
www.parenting-qa.com/

Parents' Guide to the Internet
www.ed.gov/pubs/parents/internet

The Parents at Home site
advicom.net/~jsm/moms

Parents Place
www.parentsplace.com

Parent's Resource Center
www1.tmisnet.com/~sherry/

Sesame Street Parents
www.ctw.org/parents/

Sgt. Mom's Military Family Support
www.sgtmoms.com/

Health

The American Academy of Pediatrics
Division of Publications
141 NW Point Blvd.
Elk Grove Village, IL 60007
847-228-5005
www.aap.org

The American Allergy Association
1259 El Camino, #254
Menlo Park, CA 94025
415-322-1663

American Red Cross
8111 Gatehouse Falls Rd.
Church, VA 22042
703-206-7090

Association of Maternal and Child Health Programs
1350 Connecticut Ave. NW, Ste. 803
Washington, DC 20036
202-775-0436

Be Healthy, Inc.
R.R.1, Box 172
Glen View Rd.
Waitsfield, VT 05673
800-433-5523

The Child Health Center
One Dana Rd.
Valhalla, NY 10595
914-592-2600

Dr. Paula
www.drpaula.com

Healthfinder
www.healthfinder.gov/

Insurance Information Institute
110 William St.
New York, NY 10038
212-669-9200, 800-942-4242

Kids Doctor
www.kidsdoctor.com

KidsHealth.org
www.kidshealth.org/index.html

MedWeb Pediatrics www.gen.emory.edu/medweb/
medweb.pediatrics.html

National Committee to Prevent Child Abuse
332 S. Michigan Ave.
Chicago, IL 60604
312 663-3520, 800-394-3366
Parents Anonymous (for parents under stress)
800-421-0353

Pampers Total Baby Care
totalbabycare.com/

Parents of Preemies
www.medsch.wisc.edu/childrenshosp/
  Parents_of_Preemies/index.html

Toll Free Numbers for Health Information
ns1.crisny.org/health/us/health5.html

Postpartum Depression

Depression After Delivery
P.O. Box 1282
Morrisville, PA 19067
800-944-4773, 212-295-3994

Pacific Postpartum Support Society
#104-1416 Commercial Dr.
Vancouver, BC V5L 3X9
604-255-7999

Postpartum Education for Parents
P.O. Box 6154
Santa Barbara, CA 93160
www.sbpep.org

Safety

U.S. Consumer Product Safety Commission
800-638-2772

Special Needs

American Speech-Hearing-Language Association
10801 Rockville Pike
Rockville, MD 20852
800-638-8255, 301-897-5700 (TDD)

American Sleep Disorders Association
1610 14th St. NW, Ste. 300
Rochester MN, 55901
507-287-6006

*The Association of Retarded Citizens of the
United States*
National Headquarters
P.O. Box 1047
Arlington, TX 76004
817-261-6003
thearc.org/welcome.html

CHASER
2112 North Wilkins Road
Swanton, OH 43558
Tel: 419-825-5575
Fax: 419-825-2880
www.csun.edu/~hfmth006/chaser/
CHASER@compuserve.com
For congenital heart anomalies

Epilepsy Foundation of America
800-EFA-1000

Family Village
www.familyvillage.wisc.edu/
A resource for parents of disabled children

National Down Syndrome Society
800-221-4602
www.ndss.org
email: info@ndss.org

National Lekotek Center
2100 Ridge Ave.
Evanston, IL 60201
708-328-0001, 800-366-PLAY
Enriching disabled children's lives through play

The National Parent Network on Disabilities (NPND)
1130 17th Street NW, Ste. 400
Washington, DC 20036
Tel: 202-463-2299
Fax: 202-463-9403
Website: www.npnd.org
Email: NPND@cs.net

Parents Helping Parents
The Family Resource Center
3041 Olcott St.
Santa Clara, CA 95054-3222
www.php.com.

Multiples

National Organization of Mothers of Twins Clubs, Inc.
P.O. Box 23188
Albuquerque, NM 87192-1188
505-275-0955
www.nomotc.org

Parents of Multiple Births Association of Canada
Box 234
Gormley, ON L0H 1G0
Tel: 905-888-0725
Fax: 905-888-0727
www.pomba.org
Email: office@pomba.org

INDEX

shots, distracting baby
when getting, 84
well-baby checkups, 83

E-F

ear problems, 73
having checked, 86
infections, 73, 82
encouragement, offering to
baby for accomplishments,
120
eye checkup, having if baby
squints, 86
family members,
encouraging relationship
with baby, 175
fans, to help baby sleep, 46,
47–48
feeding baby, 1–28
fussy eater, 21–22, 27
making a fun ritual, 26
night feedings, 54
setting good example, 1,
25–26
starter foods, 15–20
table manners, teaching,
23–25
fevers, 74
formula (for bottlefeeding),
5–6. *See also*
bottlefeeding
fussy eater, 21–22

G-H

gagging, baby, 75
gas, baby having, 10

gifts for baby, 11, 26
grandparents, encouraging
relationship with baby, 175
growing pains, 70
growth spurts, baby having,
27
hazardous objects, 64, 113,
116, 134
health. *See also* doctors;
medicines
medical records, keeping
track of, 85
testing baby, difficulties of,
87
well-baby checkups,
schedule of, 83
home care, when baby is ill,
77
hugs, importance of giving,
144
hyperactivity, 75

I

imitating behavior, baby,
115, 116–117, 152
independence, baby
developing, 112, 119
individuality, each baby has
own, 114
ipecac syrup, to induce
vomiting, 81
iron supplements, and
constipation, 33
irons and ironing boards,
caution regarding, 86